W9-CUQ-145

ONE POT MEALS

ONE POT MEALS

MARGARET GIN

DRAWINGS BY RIK OLSON

PITMAN

PITMAN PUBLISHING LIMITED
39 Parker Street, London WC2B 5PB

Associated Companies
Pitman Publishing Co. SA (Pty) Ltd, Johannesburg
Pitman Publishing New Zealand Ltd, Wellington
Pitman Publishing Pty Ltd, Melbourne

© 1976 Margaret Gin
Illustrations © 1976 Rik Olson
© Pitman Publishing 1977

First published in Great Britain 1977

This edition has been adapted for British readers by
Helena Radecka from the original publication by 101
Productions, San Francisco.

All rights reserved. No part of this publication may be reproduced, stored in a retrieval system, or transmitted, in
any form or by any means, electronic, mechanical, photo-
copying, recording and/or otherwise without the prior
written permission of the publishers. This book may not
be lent, resold, hired out or otherwise disposed of by way
of trade in any form of binding or cover other than that
in which it is published, without the prior consent of the
publishers. This book is sold subject to the Standard Condi-
tions of Sale of Net Books and may not be resold in the UK
below the net price.

British Library Cataloguing in Publication Data
Gin, Margaret
    One-pot cookery. — (Home and garden).
    1. Cookery
    I. Title II. Series
    641.5'89   TX840.S/

    ISBN 0–273–01101–4

Reproduced and printed by photolithography and bound in
Great Britain at The Pitman Press, Bath

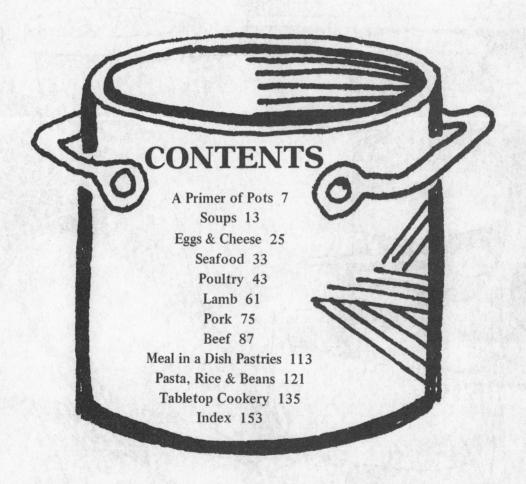

CONTENTS

A PRIMER OF POTS

One-pot cookery conserves time, fuel and fuss, while often preserving the flavor and nutritional value of foods. The tradition of one-pot cooking is probably as old as man's first efforts to cook his food and embraces most of the world's cuisines.

The Japanese cherish their "nabemono" dishes, which are one-pot meals cooked at the table over an hibachi (a portable charcoal grill — see page 135). Over the centuries the Chinese, in an effort to conserve fuel, have developed the stir-fry method of cooking to a fine art.

Many traditional European one-pot dishes are culinary classics, identified as the hallmarks of each national cuisine—the paella of Spain, pot-au-feu and bouillabaisse of France, the hochepot of Belgium and the giuvetch of Romania.

In Colonial North America, one-pot cooking was symbolized by the Dutch oven hanging over the hearth. This cast-iron vessel of many purposes was later carried west by the American pioneers and even today, in its many streamlined forms, it is indispensable to most American cooks.

Twentieth-century technology has made two significant contributions to preparing meals in a single pot: the pressure cooker, so popular during World War II, and the recently developed electric slow cooker or crockpot.

This book offers one-pot recipes from many countries, prepared in a number of ways. Where practical, several preparation methods have been listed for the same dish, i.e., a hearty stew may be cooked on top of the stove in a heavy pan, in a pressure cooker, in a slow cooker or in a wet clay cooker. Specialized cookware like fondue pots, chafing dishes, omelet pans and soufflé dishes can give variety to one-pot cookery, and recipes are given for their use. But even more useful are the commonplace basics of the *batterie de cuisine:* the all-purpose casserole, saucepan, soup pot and roasting tin.

A PRIMER OF POTS

THE PRESSURE COOKER

Treasured by World War II housewives, the pressure cooker is experiencing a revival in the modern kitchen. Busy people and cooks trying to find ways of coping with soaring fuel bills are also rediscovering the pressure cooker's versatility. Like its recent offspring, the slow cooker, it is a first-class time and money saver. And because the steam penetrates the food so quickly, valuable vitamins and minerals are retained.

When using a pressure cooker, follow the manufacturers' instructions for the use and care of their particular model. There are, however, a few basic rules for pressure cookers which apply to all models.

Do not overload the pressure cooker. When cooking soups or other liquids, the cooker should be filled to no more than half capacity. Two-thirds full is the rule of thumb for liquids combined with solids, like stews.

Reduce recipes for conventional cooking to a quarter of the time for the pressure cooker, not one-third as mentioned in many cookbooks. The cooking may always be finished not under pressure. With a stew, for example, the meat should be cooked under pressure, then the vegetables may be added and cooked after the pressure has been reduced. This preserves their flavor and freshness.

Many modern pressure cookers are equipped with variable pressure controls which allow the pressure to be adjusted according to the nature of the dish being cooked (5, 10 or 15 pounds). The pressure cooker recipes in this book have been calculated for cooking under 15-pound pressure. The majority of pressure cookers designed to cook under a fixed pressure are fitted with a 15-pound pressure valve. However, there are also fixed-pressure models on the market which cook under lower pressure. If this is the case with your cooker (check your handbook), test the food after the time specified in the recipe and if necessary continue cooking for a little while longer.

When using a pressure cooker, adjust the seasonings of the dish after the cooking is completed. The balance of flavors tends to shift in this method of cooking.

THE CASSEROLE

In this book the term casserole has been used to mean a deep dish of any heatproof material without a long handle, suitable for baking and roasting, and if flameproof, for top-of-the-stove cooking. It should have a fitted lid and, if it is made of clay or some other porous material, the surface should be sealed.

Historically the casserole has its origins in the ancient earthenware pot which, when treated with plant gum, became waterproof. Many of our modern casseroles are both heatproof and flameproof. However, a casserole which is merely heatproof can sometimes be adapted for stovetop cooking on an asbestos pad. When purchasing a new casserole for oven-to-table use, do make certain that the materials used are safe. Slow poisoning from improperly fired enamelled casseroles can occur.

THE SLOW COOKER

The slow cooker phenomenon comes as no surprise to the chef who has salvaged a poor cut of meat by simmering it slowly and basting it often. The slow cooker provides its own "moist environment," eliminating the need for basting; the cover should not be lifted until the prescribed cooking period has ended.

A high-glaze finish and the enclosure of the electric heating elements on the sides of most slow cookers prevent sticking or burning. Some models have browning units, but if yours does not, meats should be browned first in a separate pan.

For safe cooking, the temperature of the slow cooker must reach 165° within three to four hours of the beginning of the cooking time. This will minimize any growth of bacteria in the foods. Slow cookers that take too long to heat encourage bacteria growth which can cause the food to spoil.

Although the slow cooker operates at low wattage, the long cooking times make the energy consumption about the same as when the dish is cooked on an electric range. However, there is little steam generated, so valuable vitamins and minerals are retained with the slow cooker.

Some slow cookers have electric elements which may be detached for cleaning. Warm soapy water may generally be used to clean the inside of the pot. Because constructions and finishes vary, follow the manufacturer's instructions for cleaning.

While hardly a temperamental kitchen companion, certain proprieties about the slow cooker should be observed. Lifting the lid during cooking lowers the interior temperature, resulting in undercooked food or an increase in the cooking time. The cooker should be at least half full or the proper cooking temperature will not be reached. A few vegetables may be added at the end of the cooking period and cooked on high for last-minute finish. Follow the recipes precisely on this score. If excess liquid remains at end of cooking, reduce over high heat. Adjust seasonings of each dish before serving.

THE WET CLAY COOKER

The wet clay cooker, now undergoing a revival stimulated by the promotion efforts of several ambitious West German manufacturers, is an old method of cooking. The notion of clay as a protective, moisture-sealing cooking material was used by North American Indians, who wrapped wet clay around fish, threw it into the fire until it hardened, and cracked it open when the contents were presumed done. The Romans carried the use of clay for cooking vessels to its ultimate, using clay extensively though other materials were available to them.

In its modern form, the wet clay cooker is usually oval-shaped with ridges on the inside of the bottom to hold the contents slightly above the juices, thus preventing sticking. It has a fitted top with a small space for escaping steam. The wet clay

A PRIMER OF POTS

cooker has an unglazed finish throughout and must be soaked in water before each use. It may be seasoned periodically by rubbing it with garlic and adding whatever herbs are desired to the soaking water. Soaking the clay before cooking allows water to fill the "pores"; the water forms a moist haze during cooking, eliminating the need for basting or excess liquids or fats. In fact, fat may be omitted completely when cooking in a wet clay cooker, which makes it particularly useful when cooking for special diets.

The wet clay cooker has the advantage of cooking its contents in natural juices, retaining the original vitamins and nutrients, and is attractive enough for oven-to-table presentation. Avoid sudden temperature changes, remembering to start with a cold oven and to add warm liquids only after the contents have been warmed. Set the finished dish on a towel rather than a cold stone or metal surface.

As recommended by the manufacturer, use the wet clay cooker only in the oven. Even an asbestos pad is ineffective in converting some wet clay cookers to stovetop use, but a dish may be browned in the oven by removing the lid for the last 10 minutes of the cooking period. Wash thoroughly with warm soapy water after each use. Store the wet clay cooker with lid turned upside down to allow "breathing" between each use.

THE FRYING PAN

The frying pan is a catchall term used to describe a wide range of utensils of different shapes and sizes. In the mid-19th century, the frying pan was known as a "spider" and came equipped with tapered legs and a long handle; when the kitchen range became a culinary fact of life, the legs were cut off to allow the pan to rest directly on the heat source.

Before embarking on one of the recipes in this book which recommend using a frying pan, check that the pan you intend to use is large and deep enough. Some of the recipes call for the ingredients to be cooked covered and in this case a frying pan equipped with a lid should be used.

Frying pans come in many materials: cast iron, aluminium, stainless steel, copper, rolled or carbon steel, porcelain enamelware, non-stick finishes and heat-resistant glass. If using a frying pan of cast iron or rolled or carbon steel, follow the directions for its care at the end of this chapter.

THE OMELET PAN

The omelet pan is a type of frying pan with a long handle and sloping sides to facilitate sliding the omelet from the pan. Many chefs consider it a necessity, but a heavy, well-seasoned frying pan may also be effectively used for preparing omelets. Traditionally the French omelet pan is made of carbon steel, but today's market offers models in cast iron, aluminium, stainless steel, porcelain enamelware and the new non-stick surfaces. Carbon steel or cast-iron pans should be seasoned and cared for according to the directions at the end of this chapter.

THE STOCKPOT OR SOUP POT

The traditional stockpot or soup pot is taller than its diameter, thus reducing evaporation by exposing a small surface to the air. The height of the pot also allows the ingredients to boil up through the simmering stock. However, a large saucepan may always be substituted for a stockpot or soup pot. The stockpot is more versatile than it appears at first glance. With a rack it can be converted to a steamer.

THE SOUFFLÉ DISH

The soufflé dish, startling in its simplicity, is the perfect oven-to-table item. It should have straight sides, ridged on the outside and a flat bottom. Its capacity may vary from one pint (individual ramekins are much smaller) to several pints. Determine the capacity of yours by measuring the amount of liquid it holds up to the indentation line.

In several of the following recipes, a deep baking dish or ovenproof casserole may be substituted for the soufflé dish. However, even the plainest soufflé dish is so attractive that a dozen other table-top uses come to mind. The usual precautions against sudden temperature changes apply to soufflé dishes (see Wet Clay Cooker).

CARE OF ROLLED OR CARBON STEEL AND CAST-IRON COOKWARE

Carbon or rolled steel and cast-iron cookware require seasoning and special care. To season a new pot, first wash it thoroughly with detergent and hot water. Rinse well and dry the pot over heat. Then rub the inside with cooking oil, such as peanut or corn oil, and place it over high heat for one minute. Rinse in hot water and dry over heat. Rub with oil again and wipe out excess oil with paper toweling. Repeat oil application. Place over heat and wipe out with paper toweling. Repeat until paper remains clean, then rinse in hot water and dry over heat. Rub lightly with oil before storing. After each use, wash immediately with hot water and a stiff brush and dry over heat. Never use a metal scouring pad. Reseason with oil as needed.

SOUPS

TUSCAN BEAN SOUP

Serves 6 to 8
2 tablespoons olive oil
1 clove garlic, finely chopped
1 onion, chopped
1 carrot, chopped
1 celery rib, chopped
2 leeks, chopped
1 sprig rosemary, finely chopped
1 fresh green chili pepper, seeded and finely
   chopped, or
1 dried red chili pepper, seeded and crushed
1 pound dried white beans, washed,
   soaked overnight and drained
1 ham bone, cracked
salt and freshly ground pepper to taste
garnish:
   6 to 8 tablespoons grated Parmesan cheese
   1 onion, thinly sliced

Top-of-the-Stove Method
Heat oil in a large soup pot and sauté garlic, onion, carrot, celery, leeks, rosemary and chili pepper until just browned. Add beans, ham bone and 5 pints water; simmer, covered, for 2 hours. Season with salt and pepper. Remove ham bone and rub half the beans through a fine sieve (or purée in a blender). Return purée to the soup and heat through. Serve in soup bowls, garnished with cheese and onion.

Slow Cooker Method
Sauté garlic, onion, carrot, celery, leeks, rosemary and chili pepper in oil until just browned in a frying pan or slow cooker with a browning unit. Combine with beans, ham bone and 3-1/4 pints water in a slow cooker. Cover and cook on high 2 hours. Turn heat to low and cook, covered, 8 to 10 hours. Season with salt and pepper and proceed as directed for top-of-the-stove method.

13

SOUPS

MINESTRONE, MILANESE STYLE

Serves 6 to 8

1/4 pound salt pork, diced
1 clove garlic, finely chopped
1 onion, thinly sliced
2 sprigs parsley, chopped
3 ounces small dried white beans, washed,
  soaked overnight and drained
2 potatoes, peeled and cubed
2 carrots, diced
2 celery ribs, sliced
2 medium-sized courgettes, thinly sliced
2 large ripe tomatoes, peeled and chopped
1 small head cabbage, shredded
1 pound fresh peas, shelled
3 ounces rice
salt and freshly ground pepper to taste
1 tablespoon chopped basil
garnish: grated Parmesan cheese
accompaniment: crusty French bread

Top-of-the-Stove Method

In a soup pot sauté salt pork, garlic, onion and parsley over medium heat. Add beans and 5 pints of water. Put remaining vegetables into pot, except for cabbage and peas; bring to a boil. Lower heat, cover and simmer for 1-1/2 hours. Add cabbage, peas and rice and cook for 20 minutes, or until rice is tender. Add salt, pepper and basil, top with grated Parmesan and serve in individual bowls, accompanied by French bread.

Slow Cooker Method

Sauté the salt pork, garlic, onion and parsley in a frying pan or slow cooker with a browning unit. Combine with all remaining ingredients, except cabbage, peas, rice and basil, and 3-1/4 pints water in a slow cooker. Cover and cook on high 2 hours. Turn heat to low and cook, covered, 8 hours. Add cabbage, peas and rice and cook on high 30 minutes or until rice is tender. Serve as directed for top-of-the-stove method.

HAM AND LENTIL SOUP

Serves 6
3/4 pound brown lentils
1/2 pound ham, diced
1 onion, coarsely chopped
1 bay leaf
2 celery ribs, coarsely chopped
1 clove garlic, finely chopped
salt and freshly ground pepper to taste

Top-of-the-Stove Method
Combine all the ingredients with 3-1/4 pints water in a soup pot and bring to a boil. Reduce heat and simmer, covered, for 1-1/2 to 2 hours. Adjust seasonings and serve.

Slow Cooker Method
Combine all ingredients with 3-1/4 pints water in a slow cooker. Cook on low, covered, 8 to 10 hours. Adjust seasonings and serve.

Variation The soup may be served puréed. Blend 2 cups at a time in the blender, return to the soup pot and heat through.

SALT COD SOUP

Serves 6
1 pound salt cod, soaked in water to cover for
   2 hours and drained
3 tablespoons olive oil
2 onions, thinly sliced
2 cloves garlic, finely chopped
1 bay leaf
2 sprigs thyme, or
1 teaspoon dried thyme
1 celery rib, chopped
4 tablespoons chopped parsley
1 pound ripe tomatoes, peeled and chopped
scant 1/2 pint dry white wine
4 potatoes, peeled and quartered
freshly ground pepper to taste
garnish: chopped parsley and grated
   Parmesan cheese
accompaniment: crusty French bread

Cut cod into 2-1/2-inch pieces; set aside. Heat oil in soup pot or large saucepan and sauté onions and garlic until golden. Add bay leaf, thyme, celery, parsley and tomatoes and simmer for 10 minutes. Add wine, potatoes, reserved cod and 2-1/2 pints water; simmer for about 30 minutes. Season with pepper. Serve garnished with parsley and cheese and accompany with French bread.

SOUPS

PESTO SOUP

Serves 6 to 8

1 pound small dried white beans, washed, soaked
    overnight and drained
1 potato, peeled and diced
2 carrots, diced
2 leeks, diced
2 large tomatoes, peeled, seeded and diced
1/4 pound green beans, diced
2 courgettes, diced
2 sage leaves, finely chopped, or
1/4 teaspoon powdered sage
1 teaspoon salt
1/2 teaspoon freshly ground pepper
2 ounces vermicelli

Pesto Sauce

3 cloves garlic, finely chopped
6 basil leaves, finely chopped
6 to 8 tablespoons grated Parmesan cheese
4 tablespoons olive oil

Top-of-the-Stove Method

Place beans in a soup pot with 5 pints of water
and bring to a boil. Skim off any scum that appears
on the surface, lower heat, cover and simmer 1
hour. Add the potato, carrots, leeks, tomatoes,
green beans, courgettes, sage, salt and pepper and
continue simmering, covered, for another hour.
Add the vermicelli and cook for 15 minutes. Mix
the garlic, basil, Parmesan cheese and olive oil.
Remove the soup from the heat and stir in the
sauce. Serve immediately.

Slow Cooker Method

Combine all ingredients except vermicelli and sauce
in a slow cooker with 3-1/4 pints water. Cover and
cook on high 2 hours. Turn heat to low and cook,
covered, 8 hours. Add vermicelli, turn on high and
cook, covered, 30 minutes. Combine sauce ingredients, stir into soup and serve.

CHICKEN AND CORN CHOWDER

Serves 6
2 slices bacon, diced
1 onion, chopped
1 3-pound fryer chicken, cut up
1 bay leaf
1 teaspoon salt
1/2 teaspoon white pepper
1 pound fresh or frozen corn kernels
2 ribs celery, chopped
1/2 pint evaporated milk
garnish:
    2 hard-boiled eggs, chopped
    chopped parsley

In soup pot or large saucepan fry bacon just to release fat; remove bacon bits with a slotted spoon and sauté onions in drippings until golden. Place chicken in the pot and add 5 pints water. Bring to a rapid boil and skim any surface scum. Add bay leaf, salt and pepper. Lower heat and simmer covered for 1 hour. Remove chicken pieces; add corn kernels and celery and return bacon to the pot. Continue simmering covered for 30 minutes. Meanwhile, bone chicken and discard bones and fat (or save for chicken stock). Dice meat and return to the pot with the evaporated milk. Heat through and serve in warmed soup bowls, garnished with chopped eggs and parsley.

CHICKEN-NOODLE SOUP

Serves 4 to 6
1 3-pound whole fryer chicken, with giblets
1 celery rib, with leaves
2 carrots
1 onion, stuck with 2 cloves
1 bay leaf
8 ounces egg noodles
2 sprigs parsley, chopped
salt and freshly ground pepper to taste

In a soup pot combine chicken, celery, carrots, onion and bay leaf with 5 pints water. Bring to a boil, skim off any surface scum, lower heat, cover and simmer 1-1/2 hours. Remove chicken, strain broth and return broth to pot. Add noodles and continue cooking, uncovered, over medium heat for 10 minutes. Add parsley, salt and pepper. Chicken may be cut up and served separately, or boned, diced and returned to pot.

Variations
• For chicken-rice soup, substitute 6 ounces rice for noodles and cook for 20 minutes.
• For chicken-vegetable soup, chop the vegetables and add 1 large tomato, peeled, seeded and diced; do not strain broth.

SOUPS

HAITIAN CHICKEN-IN-THE-POT

Serves 4 to 6
1 3-1/2- to 4-pound whole fryer chicken
1 pound ham hocks
1/4 pint fresh orange juice
1 onion, stuck with 2 cloves
2 carrots, halved
1 small head cabbage, cut in wedges
1/2 pound small courgettes
1 celery rib, halved
2 tablespoons vinegar

Top-of-the-Stove Method
In a soup pot combine the chicken, ham hocks, orange juice and onion with water to cover (about 5 pints). Bring to a rapid boil and skim any surface scum. Lower heat, cover and simmer for 1 hour. Add carrots, cabbage, courgettes, celery and vinegar and simmer for 30 minutes. Remove the meats and vegetables and place on a warm platter. Strain broth and serve separately.

Pressure Cooker Method
In a pressure cooker combine the chicken, ham hocks, orange juice and onion with water to cover, no more than two-thirds capacity. Cover and bring to full pressure. When steam appears, reduce heat and cook on low 15 minutes. Reduce pressure completely, uncover and add carrots, cabbage, courgettes, celery and vinegar. Cover and simmer for 30 minutes, not under pressure. Let stand covered 10 to 15 minutes to blend flavors. Remove the meats and vegetables and place on a warm platter. Strain broth and serve separately.

POT-AU-FEU

Serves 8 to 10
1 beef shin bone
1 3-pound beef brisket or silverside
1 bay leaf
2 sprigs parsley
2 sprigs thyme, or
1 teaspoon dried thyme
1 whole plump chicken, about 4 pounds
1 pound chicken giblets
6 carrots, halved
3 leeks, white part only
2 onions, each stuck with 2 cloves
3 turnips, quartered
3 celery ribs with some leaves, halved
salt and freshly ground pepper to taste
accompaniments:
    pickles and horseradish
    French bread and unsalted butter

Top-of-the-Stove Method
In a soup pot, slowly bring beef bone and meat to a boil in 6-1/2 pints water. Skim off any surface scum and add bay leaf, parsley and thyme. Lower heat and simmer covered for 1-1/2 hours. Add chicken, giblets, carrots, leeks, onions, turnips and celery. Bring to a boil, cover, lower heat and simmer for 45 minutes or until chicken is tender. Season with salt and pepper. Put meats and chicken on a platter with the giblets; surround with vegetables and keep warm. Strain the broth, skimming off fat, and serve separately in cups. Slice meat and serve accompanied with pickles and horseradish. Serve with French bread and butter.

Slow Cooker Method
Combine all ingredients with only 5 pints water and cook on low, covered, for 8 to 10 hours. Serve as directed for top-of-the-stove method.

SOUPS

MULLIGATAWNY

Serves 6
1-1/2 pounds stewing lamb, cut into
  1/2-inch dice
4 tablespoons butter
1 onion, finely chopped
1 tablespoon curry powder
2 tablespoons flour
2 ounces brown lentils
2 tart apples, peeled and diced
1 green pepper, diced
2 carrots, diced
1 teaspoon sugar
1/2 teaspoon ground mace
1/4 teaspoon ground cloves
salt and freshly ground pepper to taste
1/2 pint coconut milk, following
accompaniment: freshly cooked rice

Top-of-the-Stove Method
Brown the meat in the butter in a soup pot; add onion, curry powder and flour and cook and stir for 2 minutes. Add 5 pints water and remaining ingredients except for coconut milk. Bring to a boil, lower heat and simmer for 1-1/2 hours. Add coconut milk and heat through; do not boil. Serve in individual soup bowls with rice to be added, as much as desired, to each serving.

Slow Cooker Method
Brown the meat in butter in a frying pan or slow cooker with a browning unit. Add onion, curry powder and flour and cook and stir for 2 minutes. Combine with remaining ingredients, except coconut milk, and 3-1/4 pints water in a slow cooker. Cover and cook on low 8 to 10 hours. Add coconut milk, heat through and serve with rice.

Coconut Milk
For each cup of coconut milk needed, combine 1 cup unsweetened grated coconut and 1 cup milk in a pan and bring to a boil. Remove from heat, cool and press through a sieve.

VEGETABLE AND BEEF BARLEY SOUP

Serves 6
2 pounds lean beef short ribs
1 pound tomatoes, peeled and chopped
1 teaspoon salt
1 bay leaf
1/4 pound green beans, cut into 1-inch lengths
1/4 pound fresh or frozen corn kernels
1 onion, chopped
3 ounces pearl barley
1/2 teaspoon dried oregano
1/2 teaspoon dried basil
1 clove garlic, crushed

Place short ribs, tomatoes, salt and bay leaf in a large soup pot; add 3-1/4 pints water. Cover and bring to a rapid boil; skim any surface scum. Reduce heat and simmer, covered, for 2 hours. Add remaining ingredients and simmer 1 hour, or until meat is tender. Remove short ribs from soup, cut meat from bones, dice meat and add to soup; heat through. Skim surface fat again before serving.

HUNGARIAN MEATBALL SOUP

Serves 4
1 pound lean minced beef
2 ounces fresh bread crumbs
1 egg, beaten
salt and freshly ground pepper to taste
1 onion, thinly sliced
2 tablespoons butter
1 teaspoon paprika
2 medium-size potatoes, peeled and diced
garnish:
    sour cream or plain yogurt
    chopped parsley

Combine the beef, bread crumbs, egg, salt and pepper. Shape into 1-inch balls. In a saucepan sauté the onion in butter until soft, then add the paprika and 1-1/2 pints water. Bring to a rapid boil, lower heat and add meatballs and potatoes. Cover and simmer 30 minutes. Ladle into soup bowls, top each with a spoonful of sour cream or yogurt and sprinkle parsley on top.

SOUPS

OXTAIL AND VEGETABLE SOUP

Serves 6
3 pounds oxtails, disjointed and
    parboiled 5 minutes
1 bay leaf
1 onion, chopped
2 leeks, chopped
2 celery ribs with leaves, chopped
3 carrots, diced
3 turnips, diced
3 beetroots, diced
2 large ripe tomatoes, peeled and chopped
1/2 pound cabbage, chopped, or
1/4 pound spinach or Swiss chard, chopped
2 sprigs parsley, chopped
1 teaspoon salt
1/2 teaspoon freshly ground pepper
accompaniment: French bread

Place oxtails in a large soup pot with 5 pints water. Bring to boil and skim off any surface scum. Add remaining ingredients, lower heat, cover and simmer for 1-1/2 hours. Adjust seasonings and remove bay leaf. Serve with French bread.

SOPA DE ALBONDIGAS
(Mexican Meatball Soup)

Serves 4 to 6
1/2 pound each lean minced beef and pork
4 tablespoons rice
1/2 teaspoon compound chili powder
1 teaspoon salt
1/2 teaspoon freshly ground pepper
1/4 teaspoon ground cumin
1 egg
1 onion, chopped
1 clove garlic, finely chopped
3 tablespoons olive oil
3-1/4 pints beef stock
1/2 pound ripe tomatoes, peeled and chopped
garnish: chopped parsley or coriander
accompaniment: French bread

Combine the beef, pork, rice, seasonings and egg. Shape into small balls the size of a walnut. Set aside. Sauté the onion and garlic in olive oil until golden. Add the stock and tomatoes. Bring to a rapid boil, drop in meatballs and cook, covered, over medium heat for 25 minutes. Ladle into warmed soup bowls and garnish with parsley or coriander. Serve with French bread.

SCOTCH BROTH

Serves 6 to 8
1 leftover lamb bone, with some meat remaining, or
2 pounds lamb shoulder or neck
1 onion, diced
2 carrots, diced
1 celery rib with some leaves, diced
4 tablespoons chopped parsley
1 bay leaf
1/4 teaspoon cayenne pepper
1 teaspoon dried thyme
3 ounces pearl barley
salt and freshly ground pepper to taste

Put the lamb bone, shoulder or neck in a soup pot with 5 pints of water. Bring to a rapid boil and skim any surface scum. Add remaining ingredients, bring back to a boil and simmer, covered, for 2 hours. Remove lamb bone, scrape and dice meat, and return meat to pot. Serve very hot in deep soup bowls.

EGGS & CHEESE

BAKED EGGS WITH PARMESAN CHEESE

Serves 3 or 4
2 tablespoons butter
6 to 8 tablespoons grated Parmesan cheese
6 eggs
scant 1/2 pint plain yogurt
salt and pepper to taste
6 slices rye bread toast
optional accompaniment: sliced tomatoes and
    pepper strips in vinaigrette

Butter a shallow baking dish with 1 teaspoon of
the butter and sprinkle half the cheese over the
bottom. Carefully break the eggs into the dish,
spacing them evenly over the cheese surface, and
spoon the yogurt over the eggs. Salt and pepper
lightly. Sprinkle remaining cheese on top of eggs.
Dot with remaining butter and bake in a preheated
350° oven for 15 minutes. Serve over toast with
sliced tomatoes and pepper strips, if desired.

COURGETTE, POTATO AND CHEESE CASSEROLE

Serves 4
1 pound courgettes, thinly sliced
3 potatoes, peeled and thinly sliced
6 ounces mild Cheddar cheese, grated
2 ounces fresh bread crumbs
6 to 8 tablespoons chopped parsley
2 cloves garlic, finely chopped
3 tablespoons olive oil
3 tablespoons butter
salt and freshly ground pepper to taste

Butter an earthenware 2-1/2-pint casserole or baking
dish and layer with one-third of the courgette
and potato slices. Sprinkle with one-third of the
cheese, bread crumbs, parsley, garlic, salt, pepper
and drizzle with 1 tablespoon of the oil. Repeat
each layer twice, drizzling each with oil. Dot top
with butter and pour 4 tablespoons water over all.
Cover and bake in a preheated 350° oven for 1
hour

EGGS & CHEESE

CHEESE AND CORN PIE

Serves 8
2 onions, chopped
4 tablespoons corn oil
2 large tomatoes, peeled and diced
4 ounces unbleached white flour
3 ounces cornmeal
1 tablespoon baking powder
1 teaspoon salt
2 tablespoons sugar
1 egg
8 fluid ounces milk
2 ounces butter, melted
1 1-pound can creamed-style corn
3 eggs, separated and at room temperature
1/2 pound mild Cheddar cheese, grated

Sauté onions in oil until transparent; add tomatoes and cook for 5 minutes. Set aside. Sift together flour, cornmeal, baking powder, salt and sugar. Add whole egg, milk and butter to flour mixture and blend well. Add corn, egg yolks, cheese and onion-tomato mixture to flour mixture. Beat egg whites until stiff but not dry and fold into flour mixture. Bake in a buttered 3-pint casserole in a preheated 300° oven for 1 hour, or until firm.

ASPARAGUS-HAM-AND-CHEESE TORTE

Serves 6
2 pounds asparagus, thinly sliced on diagonal
    and parboiled 2 minutes
3/4 pound cooked ham, shredded
3 ounces Cheddar cheese, grated
salt and freshly ground pepper to taste
3/4 pint milk
3 eggs, beaten
dash of freshly grated nutmeg

Generously butter a 3-pint casserole or baking dish and make layers of half the asparagus, ham and cheese. Season with salt and pepper. Repeat layers. Combine milk and eggs and pour over all. Sprinkle with nutmeg and place in a preheated 350° oven for 35 minutes, or until set.

Variations
In place of asparagus, use:
• 2 pounds courgettes, sliced and parboiled 2 minutes
• 2 pounds spinach, blanched and chopped
• 2 pounds broccoli, trimmed, coarsely chopped and parboiled 2 minutes
In place of ham, use:
• cooked shredded chicken or turkey
• cooked shrimps, prawns or crab meat

MINCED BEEF, SPINACH AND EGGS

Serves 4
2 tablespoons each butter and olive oil
1 small onion, chopped
1 clove garlic, finely chopped
1/2 pound lean minced beef
1 pound spinach, blanched, chopped and
   well drained
6 eggs, lightly beaten
salt and freshly ground pepper to taste

Heat a frying pan over medium heat, add butter and oil; sauté the onion and garlic for 1 minute. Add the beef, stirring constantly until the redness disappears. Combine the spinach and eggs and pour over the meat and onion mixture. Cook until the bottom begins to set, turning the uncooked eggs into the center with a spatula. Continue cooking until the eggs are almost set; do not overcook. Season with salt and pepper.

CHICKEN LIVERS AND EGGS ON TOAST

Serves 4
3 tablespoons butter
1/2 pound chicken livers, halved
2 tablespoons chopped onion
1 teaspoon tomato paste
5 tablespoons dry white wine
4 eggs
freshly made toast, preferably French bread
salt and freshly ground pepper to taste
freshly grated nutmeg

In a frying pan over moderate heat, melt butter. Sauté the chicken livers with onion until livers lose their redness, about 5 minutes. Blend in tomato paste and wine. Break eggs into pan, one at a time, being careful not to break yolks. Cover and cook over low heat for 2 minutes, or until whites are just firm and yolks are soft. Serve hot on toast and sprinkle with nutmeg.

EGGS & CHEESE

MEAT-AND-TOMATO CAKE

Serves 6
1 pound lean minced beef
1 large onion, chopped
1 clove garlic, finely chopped
2 tablespoons olive oil
1/2 teaspoon each salt and freshly
    ground pepper
2 large tomatoes, peeled and chopped
5 tablespoons finely chopped parsley
1 teaspoon ground cumin
2 tablespoons chopped mint, or
2 teaspoons dried mint
4 eggs, beaten

In a frying pan brown beef, onion and garlic in oil;
add salt, pepper, tomatoes, parsley, cumin and mint.
Cook over low heat, stirring constantly. Blend eggs
into meat mixture and cook over low heat until
eggs are set. Cut into wedges to serve.

RICE FRITTATA

Serves 6
6 ounces rice, cooked
1 pound cooked vegetables, chopped (courgettes,
    spinach and/or asparagus may be used)
2 tablespoons chopped spring onions
1 teaspoon dried oregano
2 teaspoons chopped basil, or
3/4 teaspoon dried basil
6 to 8 tablespoons grated Parmesan cheese
3 ounces mild Cheddar cheese, grated
4 eggs, beaten
4 tablespoons olive oil
salt and freshly ground pepper to taste

Combine all ingredients and pour into a buttered
3-pint baking dish. Bake in preheated 350° oven for
25 minutes, or until eggs are set. Cut into squares
and serve hot or cold.

Variations Add 6 to 8 tablespoons chopped cooked
ham, chicken or veal before baking.

CHEESE SOUFFLÉ

Serves 4 to 6
1/4 pound butter
2 ounces unbleached white flour
3/4 pint milk
6 ounces Cheddar cheese, grated
1/2 teaspoon paprika
1 teaspoon dry mustard
8 eggs, separated and at room temperature

Melt butter in a double boiler; blend in flour until the mixture is smooth. Stir in milk slowly and cook until the mixture thickens. Blend in grated cheese and seasonings. Stir until the cheese melts, and remove from heat. Beat the egg yolks well and stir into the cheese mixture. Beat the egg whites until stiff but not dry and fold carefully into the mixture. Turn into a buttered 3-pint soufflé dish or deep casserole. Place in a pan of hot water and bake in a preheated 350° oven 50 to 60 minutes, or until golden brown. Serve at once.

VEGETABLE SOUFFLÉ

Serves 4 to 6
1 small onion, chopped
3 ounces butter
5 tablespoons quick-cooking tapioca
12 fluid ounces milk
4 eggs, separated and at room temperature
1/2 teaspoon salt
pinch of freshly ground pepper
10 to 12 ounces chopped cooked vegetable, such as spinach, broccoli, cauliflower, green beans, peas, carrots, corn, courgettes, asparagus, artichoke hearts or any combination
3 ounces sharp Cheddar cheese, grated

In a saucepan sauté onion in butter for 5 minutes. Add tapioca, milk, egg yolks and salt and pepper. Cook over medium heat and bring to a boil, stirring constantly until thickened. Remove from heat, add vegetable and cheese and stir until cheese is melted. Beat egg whites until stiff but not dry. Fold egg whites gently into vegetable mixture and pour into a buttered 3-pint soufflé dish or casserole. Set in a pan of hot water and bake at 350° for 1 hour. Serve immediately.

EGGS & CHEESE

HAM, CHEESE AND ASPARAGUS SOUFFLÉ

Serves 4
8 ounces cooked ham, diced
2 tablespoons chopped parsley
4 ounces asparagus, cooked and coarsely cut
8 ounces elbow macaroni, cooked
4 ounces Gruyère cheese, grated
4 eggs, separated and at room temperature
8 fluid ounces double cream
1/2 teaspoon freshly grated nutmeg
1/2 teaspoon salt
1/4 teaspoon freshly ground pepper

Fit a lightly buttered, 2-1/2 pint soufflé dish with a 6-inch-wide band of foil or greaseproof paper, doubled to form a standing collar extending 2 inches above the rim. Butter the collar. Combine the ham, parsley, asparagus, macaroni and cheese. Beat the egg yolks and combine with the cream, nutmeg, salt and pepper. Blend yolk mixture with the ham mixture. In a separate bowl, beat the egg whites until stiff but not dry and fold into the ham mixture. Transfer into the prepared soufflé dish, set in a pan of hot water and bake in a preheated 375° oven for 35 to 40 minutes, or until puffed and brown. Remove the collar and serve the soufflé immediately.

Variations Substitute diced cooked chicken, turkey, pork, veal or lamb for the ham.

CURD CHEESE OMELET

Serves 4
4 tablespoons olive oil
4 tablespoons chopped onion
1 tablespoon chopped basil, or
1 teaspoon dried basil
3/4 pound ripe tomatoes, peeled and chopped
1/2 pound curd cheese (cottage cheese may be substituted)
5 tablespoons grated Parmesan cheese
salt and freshly ground pepper to taste
2 tablespoons chopped parsley
6 eggs
3 tablespoons butter

Heat oil in an omelet or frying pan. Add onion, basil and tomatoes and cook briskly for 20 minutes; remove to a side dish. Beat curd cheese with 2 tablespoons of the Parmesan, the salt and parsley until smooth; set aside. Beat eggs with remaining Parmesan and season with salt and pepper; set aside. Heat the butter in omelet pan. Pour in egg mixture and cook over low heat until puffy. Pour cheese mixture down middle and fold over both sides. Remove to a warm platter. Cover with tomato sauce and serve immediately.

CHEESE AND RICE OMELET

Serves 4
6 eggs, separated
4 tablespoons milk
5 tablespoons rice, cooked
salt and freshly ground pepper to taste
2 tablespoons each butter and corn oil
6 ounces mild Cheddar cheese, grated
3 tablespoons or more diced sweet green pepper
accompaniment: sliced tomatoes

Combine egg yolks and milk and beat well. Add rice and salt and pepper. Beat egg whites until stiff but not dry and fold into yolk mixture. Heat butter and oil in an omelet pan, pour in egg-rice mixture and cook over low heat until puffy. Sprinkle with grated cheese and peppers; place under grill briefly until cheese melts. Cut into wedges and serve immediately.

BASQUE OMELET

Serves 4
1 2-ounce can anchovy fillets,
   drained and cut in small pieces
8 eggs, lightly beaten
3 tablespoons each butter and olive oil
1 sweet green pepper, thinly sliced
1 sweet red pepper, thinly sliced
1 onion, thinly sliced
2 large firm ripe tomatoes, peeled, seeded and
   diced
salt and freshly ground pepper to taste

Mix the anchovy pieces with the eggs; set aside. In a frying pan heat butter and oil over medium heat and sauté the peppers and onions for 5 minutes, or until vegetables are just wilted. Add the tomatoes and cook 5 minutes. Pour the egg-anchovy mixture over the vegetables and scramble until almost set and puffy. Stop scrambling and cook for 1-1/2 to 2 minutes, or until bottom is lightly golden. Turn out onto a warm platter, season with salt and pepper and serve immediately.

SEAFOOD

FISH STEW, GENOA STYLE

Serves 6
4 tablespoons olive oil
2 cloves garlic
1 onion, chopped
2 anchovy fillets, finely chopped
3 sprigs parsley, chopped
1 pound ripe tomatoes, peeled and chopped
4 tablespoons finely chopped walnuts
1/2 pint dry white wine
3 pounds firm fish fillets (cod, halibut, salmon, or
    bass), cut into pieces and boned
1 bay leaf
salt and white pepper to taste
accompaniment: French bread

Heat oil in a flameproof casserole or heavy pan and sauté garlic cloves and onion; discard garlic when brown. Add anchovies, parsley and tomatoes. Combine walnuts and wine and add to casserole. Simmer 15 minutes and add fish, bay leaf, salt and pepper. Continue cooking for about 15 minutes, or until fish is just tender. Serve accompanied by French bread.

SEAFOOD

FISH AND VEGETABLE STEW WITH RICE

Serves 4 to 6
1 onion, sliced
2 tablespoons corn oil
2 large ripe tomatoes, peeled, seeded and diced
1 or more fresh green chili peppers, seeded and
    diced, or dried red chilies, seeded and crushed
2 carrots, sliced
2 small sweet potatoes, peeled and cut into
    1-inch cubes
1/2 pound cabbage, shredded (approximately
    1/2 head)
1/2 pound okra, sliced
2 pounds firm white fish fillets, such as halibut or
    turbot, cut into 1-1/2-inch pieces
salt and freshly ground pepper to taste
accompaniment: freshly cooked rice

Sauté the onion in oil in a large saucepan until
transparent. Add 1-1/2 pints water and the vegetables. Bring to a rapid boil, cover, lower heat and
simmer 40 minutes. Add the fish fillets and simmer
for 15 minutes, or until fish is just tender. Season
with salt and pepper. Serve over rice in large soup
plates.

PUERTO RICAN SEAFOOD-AND-MEAT STEW

Serves 4 to 6
2 onions, chopped
2 cloves garlic, finely chopped
1 or more fresh green chili peppers, seeded
    and chopped, or dried red chili peppers, seeded
    and crushed
2 tablespoons lard or olive oil
3/4 pound rice
2-1/2 pints chicken stock or water, heated
1 pound firm white fish fillets, cut into
    1-inch cubes
1/2 pound fresh lobster meat, cut into chunks, or
1/2 pound scallops
1/2 pound ham, cut into 1/2-inch chunks
1/4 pound chorizo sausage, sliced 1/2-inch thick
1 bay leaf
garnish:
    chopped coriander
    lemon or lime wedges

Sauté onions, garlic and chili pepper in lard for 2
minutes; then add rice and sauté 5 minutes, or
until rice is shiny. Add half of the stock and cook
over high heat until liquid is absorbed. Lower heat
to medium and add remaining stock. Place fish,
lobster or scallops, ham, chorizo and bay leaf on
top of rice. Cover and cook over low heat for 15
minutes, or until rice is tender. Serve in large
individual bowls, with coriander sprinkled over top
and lemon and lime wedges on the side.

BOUILLABAISSE

Serves 10 to 12

2 pounds ripe tomatoes, peeled, seeded and
   chopped
4 leeks, chopped
2 onions, chopped
1 carrot, chopped
3 cloves garlic, finely chopped
3 tablespoons chopped parsley
1 bay leaf
1/2 teaspoon dried thyme
1/2 teaspoon saffron threads
1 teaspoon grated orange peel
1/4 pint olive oil
1/2 pint dry white wine
2 to 3 pounds fresh lobster or crab, cut up in
   their shells
3 pounds assorted firm fresh fish fillets, such as
   red mullet, cod, halibut, perch, bass or
   mackerel, cut into 1-inch slices
12 clams or mussels in shells, well scrubbed
salt and freshly ground pepper to taste
sliced French bread
accompaniment: French bread and unsalted
   butter

Combine all the vegetables and seasonings in a large
soup pot with olive oil, wine and 3-1/4 pints water.
Bring to a rapid boil, then add lobster or crab and
cook for 8 minutes, covered. Add remaining seafood, cover and cook 8 to 10 minutes more; do not
overcook. Remove seafood to a warm serving dish;
put a slice of French bread on the bottom of each
soup bowl and pour broth over it. Serve soup and
seafood separately with additional French bread
and unsalted butter on the side.

SEAFOOD

CREAMED CODFISH ON TOAST

Serves 4
1 pound salt cod
1/2 pint single cream
1/4 pint milk
pinch of cayenne pepper
1 teaspoon flour
3 tablespoons butter, at room temperature
4 thick slices of freshly buttered, hot toast
freshly grated nutmeg
3 hard-boiled eggs, chopped
2 tablespoons chopped parsley

Soak the cod overnight in water to cover. Drain, rinse and put in a frying pan with water to cover. Bring to a boil and simmer for 10 minutes. Drain and pat dry with paper toweling. Cut in small pieces. Heat the cream and milk in the pan and add the cod. Simmer for 5 minutes and add the cayenne pepper. Mix the flour and butter into a paste and gradually add to the creamed cod mixture, stirring until thickened. Spoon over the toast. Dust with nutmeg and sprinkle with the chopped eggs and parsley.

CODFISH, POTATO AND ONION SAUTÉ

Serves 4
1 pound salt cod
2 potatoes, peeled and thinly sliced
2 onions, thinly sliced
3 tablespoons each butter and corn oil
2 cloves garlic, finely chopped
1/2 teaspoon freshly ground pepper
malt vinegar (or any mild vinegar)
chopped parsley

Soak codfish overnight in water to cover. Drain, rinse and put in a frying pan with water to cover. Bring to a boil and simmer 10 minutes. Drain and pat dry with paper toweling. Cut fish into small pieces and set aside. Heat the pan and sauté the potatoes and onions in the butter and oil for 10 minutes. Add the garlic and return the fish to the pan, cooking 10 minutes over high heat, or until the fish, potatoes and onions turn golden brown. Season with pepper. Sprinkle with vinegar and parsley.

SEAFOOD

FISH CURRY

Serves 6 to 8
1 teaspoon coriander seeds
1/2 teaspoon fennel seeds
1/4 teaspoon cumin seeds
1 small stick cinnamon
2 cardamom seeds
3 peppercorns
1/4 teaspoon cayenne pepper
1/2 teaspoon ground turmeric
2 tablespoons each butter and corn oil
2 thin slices ginger root, finely chopped, or
1/2 teaspoon ground ginger
1 small onion, sliced
3/4 pint coconut milk, page 20
2 pounds firm white fish fillets (halibut, cod or
    bass) cut into 1/2-inch by 1-inch strips
accompaniment: freshly cooked rice

Grind together coriander, fennel, cumin, cinnamon, cardamom and peppercorns; set aside. In a frying pan sauté cayenne pepper and turmeric in the butter and oil. Add ground spices, ginger and onion and continue sautéing until onion is transparent. Add coconut milk and fish and simmer 10 minutes, or until fish is tender. Serve over rice.

POACHED FISH LOAF

Serves 6 to 8
2 pounds fresh minced fish, preferably a mixture
    of a variety of fish such as flounder, eel, carp
    and halibut
4 tablespoons capers
3 tablespoons butter, at room temperature
1/2 teaspoon dried tarragon
1/4 teaspoon dried rosemary
1 teaspoon salt
1/2 teaspoon white pepper
3/4 pint dry white wine
3/4 pint water
1 onion, quartered
2 whole cloves
2 celery ribs with leaves, quartered
3 sprigs parsley
accompaniments: melted butter, prepared
    mustard, thinly sliced sweet red onions,
    lemon wedges, rye bread

Combine minced fish, capers, butter, tarragon, rosemary, salt and pepper and form into a loaf. Place on a double thickness of wet cheesecloth. Wrap roll and tie at both ends with white string; set aside. Put the remaining ingredients in a large pan. Bring to a rapid boil, lower heat and put the fish loaf in the pan. Cover and simmer gently for 40 minutes. Remove fish loaf; let rest 10 minutes and unwrap carefully. Serve with accompaniments. This dish may also be served chilled.

PRAWN JAMBALAYA

Serves 6 to 8
1 onion, chopped
2 cloves garlic, finely chopped
3 tablespoons peanut oil
1 green pepper, diced
1 pound ripe tomatoes, peeled and chopped
1/4 teaspoon cayenne pepper
1/4 teaspoon dried thyme
1/4 teaspoon ground cloves
salt and freshly ground pepper
1 pound uncooked ham, cut into 1/2-inch dice
3/4 pound rice
1 pound medium-sized prawns, shelled
   and deveined
garnish: chopped parsley

Sauté onion and garlic in oil in a large frying pan for 5 minutes. Add pepper, tomatoes, cayenne, thyme, cloves, salt, pepper and 1-1/4 pints water. Bring to a boil and add ham and rice. Cover, lower heat to simmer and cook 20 minutes. Place prawns on top, cover and cook another 10 minutes. Serve garnished with chopped parsley.

FISH PUDDING

Serves 6
1 pound sole fillets (haddock or flounder may
   be substituted)
1/2 pint coconut milk, page 20
1 teaspoon salt
1 teaspoon ground turmeric
1 clove garlic, finely chopped
1/4 teaspoon cayenne pepper
1 tablespoon paprika
1 small onion, finely chopped
5 eggs
garnish: sliced cucumbers
accompaniment: boiled potatoes

Cut fish into 1/2-inch strips and place in a buttered 1-1/2-pint baking dish. Mix the coconut milk, salt, turmeric, garlic, cayenne, paprika and chopped onion, and gradually beat in eggs, one at a time. Pour over fish. Place the dish in a pan of hot water and bake in a preheated 325° oven for 50 minutes, or until knife inserted in center comes out clean. Serve at once, garnished with cucumbers and accompanied by boiled potatoes.

SEAFOOD

FISH AND RICE CASSEROLE

Serves 3 or 4
1 pound white fish fillets (cod, halibut or sole)
4 tablespoons butter
1 onion, chopped
6 to 8 tablespoons pine nuts
6 ounces rice
3/4 pint fish stock or water
salt and white pepper to taste
1 pound fresh peas, shelled

Brown fish in 2 tablespoons of the butter in a flameproof 3-pint casserole; remove fish from casserole and set aside. Sauté onion and pine nuts in remaining 2 tablespoons of butter in the casserole for 2 minutes. Add rice and continue sautéing until rice is shiny, about 5 minutes. Pour in stock, add salt and pepper and place browned fish fillets and peas on top. Cover and place in a preheated 350° oven for 45 minutes or until rice is tender.

KEDGEREE
(Curried Baked Fish and Rice)

Serves 4
6 ounces long-grain rice, cooked
1 pound white fish (flounder, sole, halibut, or
    bass), cooked and flaked
3 ounces mild Cheddar cheese, grated
3 eggs, lightly beaten
3 tablespoons chopped spring onion
2 teaspoons curry powder
1/4 teaspoon Worcestershire sauce
pinch of cayenne pepper
salt and freshly ground pepper to taste
3 tablespoons butter
accompaniments: banana slices, chopped
    cucumber, chutney, chopped roasted peanuts

Combine all the ingredients, except the butter, and pour into a buttered 2-1/2-pint baking dish. Dot with butter and bake in a preheated 350° oven for 35 to 40 minutes, or until golden brown. Serve with accompaniments.

BAKED AVOCADO WITH CRAB

Serves 6
3 firm unpeeled avocados, halved and pitted
juice of 1 lemon
1/2 pound flaked cooked crab meat
2 tablespoons chopped chives
1 tablespoon capers
1/2 pint White Sauce, following
pinch of cayenne pepper
salt and white pepper to taste
6 to 8 tablespoons grated Cheddar cheese
2 tablespoons bread crumbs
accompaniment: crusty French bread rolls

Sprinkle cut avocados with lemon juice. Combine crab meat, chives, capers, White Sauce, cayenne, salt and pepper and fill avocados with mixture. Mix together the cheese and bread crumbs and sprinkle over the crab filling. Place the stuffed avocados in a shallow baking dish with 1/2-inch hot water and bake in a preheated 350° oven for 25 minutes. Serve with crusty rolls.

Variation Substitute for the crab meat, small cooked prawns, cooked flaked salmon or tuna, cooked diced chicken or turkey.

WHITE SAUCE

Makes 1/2 pint
2 tablespoons butter
2 tablespoons flour
1/2 pint milk
salt
white pepper
2 tablespoons double cream (optional)

In a saucepan melt butter over low heat and stir in the flour. Cook for 3 minutes. Do not brown. Stir in milk and continue cooking over low heat, stirring constantly, until sauce begins to thicken. Season with salt and pepper. For a richer white sauce, the double cream may be added before completion.

POULTRY

CHICKEN FRICASSEE WITH RICE

Serves 4

1 3-1/2- to 4-pound fryer chicken, cut up
2 tablespoons each butter and corn oil
1 onion, chopped
salt and white pepper to taste
1/2 teaspoon dried tarragon
1 pint chicken stock
6 ounces rice
1/4 pound small button mushrooms
6 to 8 small boiling onions
1 carrot, thinly sliced
1 pound fresh peas, shelled
1/2 pint double cream
3 egg yolks
garnish: chopped parsley

Top-of-the-Stove Method

In a flameproof casserole brown chicken on all sides in butter and oil over medium heat about 10 minutes. Add chopped onion, salt, pepper, tar-ragon and chicken stock. Cover and simmer for 20 minutes. Stir in rice, mushrooms, boiling onions and carrot and continue cooking over low heat for 15 minutes. Add the peas, cover and simmer 10 minutes longer. Remove pot from heat and blend cream and egg yolks gradually into chicken and rice mixture. Return to low heat and heat through. Garnish with parsley and serve.

Wet Clay Cooker Method

Combine chopped onion, salt, pepper, tarragon and only 3/4 pint chicken stock in a pre-soaked unglazed clay cooker. Stir in rice, mushrooms, boiling onions and carrot. Top with chicken pieces and drizzle with melted butter and oil. Cover and place in a cold oven. Turn oven to 400° and bake 1 hour and 15 minutes. Remove from oven, blend cream and egg yolks gradually into chicken and rice mixture and add peas. Cover and return to oven for 10 minutes. Remove from oven and let stand 10 minutes. Garnish with parsley and serve.

43

POULTRY

CHICKEN RAGOUT

Serves 3 to 4
2 tablespoons corn oil
1 onion, chopped
1 3-pound fryer chicken, cut up, with giblets
2 tablespoons chopped parsley
1 teaspoon ground cumin
3/4 pint chicken stock
2 potatoes, peeled and diced
4 tablespoons fresh lemon juice
1 egg, beaten
2 tablespoons chopped dill

Top-of-the-Stove Method (flameproof casserole or large frying pan may be used)

Heat oil and sauté onion until transparent. Add chicken parts and giblets and brown on all sides. Add parsley, cumin and stock; cover and simmer for 30 minutes. Add potatoes and cook 20 minutes or until tender. Stir in lemon juice. Take 1/2 cup of cooking liquid from pot and stir in beaten egg; return egg mixture to pot and stir constantly until thickened. Do not allow liquid to come to a boil. Stir in fresh dill just before serving.

Slow Cooker Method

Brown chicken and giblets with onion in oil in a frying pan or slow cooker with browning unit. Put potatoes in the bottom of the slow cooker and place browned chicken and onion on top. Add parsley, cumin and generous 1/2 pint stock; cover and cook on low for 6 to 8 hours. When ready to serve, stir in lemon juice. Take 1/2 cup of cooking liquid from pot and stir beaten egg into it; return egg mixture to pot and turn on high. Stirring constantly, cook until thickened. Do not allow liquid to come to a boil. Stir in fresh dill just before serving.

Wet Clay Cooker Method

Combine ingredients, using a generous 1/2 pint stock (browning is not necessary), except lemon juice, egg and dill in a pre-soaked unglazed clay cooker. Cover and place in a cold oven. Turn oven to 400° and bake 1 hour and 15 minutes. Remove from oven, uncover and stir in lemon juice. Take 1/2 cup of cooking liquid and stir beaten egg into it. Stir egg mixture into pot. Cover and let stand 10 minutes. Stir in fresh dill just before serving.

CHICKEN STEW, ITALIAN STYLE

Serves 4

1 3-1/2- to 4-pound chicken, cut up (or equivalent weight of chicken parts)
3 tablespoons olive oil
2 onions, sliced
1 teaspoon salt
1/2 teaspoon freshly ground pepper
1 celery rib, cut into small chunks
2 medium-size potatoes, peeled and diced
1/2 pound ripe tomatoes, peeled and chopped
1 teaspoon dried oregano
3 tablespoons chopped parsley
1 pound fresh peas, shelled

Oven Method (heatproof casserole may be used)

Rub the chicken or chicken parts with the olive oil
and brown with onions in a preheated 425° oven
for 15 minutes. Add other ingredients, except peas,
and 1/2 pint water. Cover the vessel with a tight-
fitting lid, lower oven to 325° and continue cooking for 45 minutes. Add the peas and cook an
additional 15 minutes.

Slow Cooker Method

Brown chicken parts in oil in a frying pan or a slow
cooker with a browning unit. Add salt, pepper and
onions and cook for another 5 minutes. Put celery
and potatoes in the bottom of the slow cooker and
top with browned chicken, onions, tomatoes, 1/4
pint water, oregano and parsley. Cover and cook on
low for 6 to 8 hours. Add peas, cover and cook on
high 15 minutes.

Pressure Cooker Method

Heat the oil in the pressure cooker and brown the
chicken parts. Add salt, pepper, onions, celery,
tomatoes, 1/2 pint water, oregano and parsley.
Cover and bring to full pressure. When steam appears, reduce heat and cook on low for 10 minutes.
Reduce pressure completely and add potatoes.
Continue cooking, covered, 10 minutes, not under
pressure. Add peas and cook 5 minutes. Let stand
covered 10 to 15 minutes to blend flavors.

POULTRY

BRUNSWICK STEW

Serves 6
2 slices bacon, diced
3 tablespoons flour
1 teaspoon salt
1/2 teaspoon freshly ground pepper
pinch of cayenne pepper
1 3- to 4-pound rabbit or chicken, cut up, with
   giblets
3 onions, thinly sliced
4 large ripe tomatoes, peeled and chopped
1 sweet red pepper, chopped
1/2 teaspoon dried thyme
1/2 pound shelled broad beans
1/2 pound fresh or frozen corn kernels
1/2 pound okra, sliced
2 tablespoons chopped parsley
1 tablespoon Worcestershire sauce

Top-of-the-Stove Method
(flameproof casserole or heavy saucepan may be used)
Cook the bacon in its own fat until rendered. Remove the bacon bits and set aside. Combine flour, salt, pepper and cayenne and dredge rabbit or chicken. Brown the pieces in the rendered fat with the onions. Add 3/4 pint boiling water, tomatoes, sweet red pepper and thyme. Cover and simmer 1 hour. Add remaining ingredients, including reserved bacon, cover and continue cooking 15 to 20 minutes or until vegetables are tender.

Slow Cooker Method

Cook the bacon in its own fat until rendered in a frying pan or slow cooker with a browning unit. Remove the bacon bits and set aside. Combine flour, salt, pepper and cayenne and dredge the rabbit or chicken. Brown the pieces in the rendered fat with the onions. Add a generous 1/2 pint boiling water, tomatoes, sweet red pepper and thyme to a slow cooker with the meat. Cover and cook on low 6 to 8 hours. Add remaining ingredients including reserved bacon, cover and cook on high 25 minutes or until vegetables are tender.

Pressure Cooker Method

In a pressure cooker cook the bacon in its own fat until rendered. Remove the bacon bits and set aside. Combine flour, salt, pepper and cayenne and dredge rabbit or chicken. Brown the pieces in the rendered fat with the onions. Add 1-1/4 pints water, tomatoes, red pepper and thyme. Cover and bring to full pressure. When steam appears, reduce heat and cook on low 15 minutes. Reduce pressure completely, uncover and add remaining ingredients, including reserved bacon. Cover and cook 10 minutes, not under pressure. Let stand, covered, 10 to 15 minutes to blend flavors.

47

POULTRY

CHICKEN SAUTÉ, HUNTER'S STYLE

Serves 4 to 6
1 onion, sliced
1 carrot, chopped
1 celery rib, chopped
4 tablespoons butter
1-1/2 tablespoons olive oil
1 3-pound fryer chicken, cut up
1/4 pint dry white wine
1 pound ripe tomatoes, peeled and chopped
salt and freshly ground pepper to taste
pinch of ground cinnamon
2 whole cloves
1/2 pound small button mushrooms

In a large flameproof casserole, sauté onion, carrot and celery in butter and oil. Add chicken pieces and brown lightly. Add wine and tomatoes and salt and pepper lightly. Sprinkle with cinnamon and toss in cloves. Continue cooking, uncovered, over medium heat for 45 minutes, or until chicken is tender. Add mushrooms for last 10 minutes of cooking period.

CHICKEN À LA KING

Serves 6
1/4 pound button mushrooms, sliced
1 green pepper, thinly sliced
4 tablespoons butter
3/4 pint White Sauce, page 41
6 to 8 tablespoons dry sherry
1-1/2 teaspoons dried tarragon
pinch cayenne pepper
1/2 teaspoon salt
1/4 teaspoon white pepper
4 egg yolks
6 to 8 tablespoons double cream
1 pound cooked chicken, cubed
2 tablespoons chopped pimiento
accompaniment: freshly cooked rice,
    toast triangles or vol-au-vent cases

In a heavy saucepan sauté mushrooms and pepper in the butter for 5 minutes. Add White Sauce, sherry, tarragon, cayenne and salt and pepper. Bring just to a boil, stirring constantly. Combine egg yolks with cream and stir into the sauce. Add the chicken and heat through without boiling. Sprinkle with pimiento and serve over rice, toast or in vol-au-vent cases.

Variation Substitute turkey for the chicken.

COUNTRY CAPTAIN

Serves 6
1 3-pound fryer chicken, cut up
3 tablespoons flour
1 teaspoon salt
1/4 teaspoon freshly ground pepper
3 tablespoons each butter and corn oil
1 clove garlic, finely chopped
1 onion, chopped
1 green pepper, chopped
1-1/2 teaspoons curry powder
1 pound ripe tomatoes, peeled and chopped
4 tablespoons currants
accompaniments:
    freshly cooked rice
    chutney
    blanched toasted almonds
    chopped spring onions

Dust the chicken pieces with the flour, salt and pepper. In a large frying pan brown chicken in butter and oil on all sides. Remove from pan and set aside. Add the garlic, onion, pepper and curry powder to the frying pan; cook for 3 minutes over low heat. Add the tomatoes and return the chicken pieces, skin side up, to the pan. Cover and simmer for 30 minutes, or until chicken is tender. Stir in currants. Serve over rice with accompaniments.

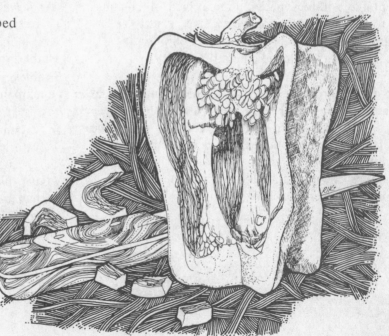

POULTRY

CHICKEN CURRY WITH COCONUT SAUCE

Serves 4
2 onions, sliced
2 cloves garlic, finely chopped
2 tablespoons butter
1 or more tablespoons curry powder
1 teaspoon compound chili powder
1 teaspoon salt
generous 1/2 pint coconut milk, page 20
1 3-pound fryer chicken, cut up
1 pound potatoes, peeled and cut into 1-inch cubes
6 to 8 tablespoons chopped roasted peanuts
garnish: chopped coriander, spring onions and
    seeded and chopped cucumbers

In a flameproof casserole sauté onions and garlic in
butter until soft. Stir in curry and chili powders
and salt. Add scant 1/2 pint coconut milk, the
chicken and the potatoes. Cover and simmer for 30
minutes, or until chicken is tender. Add the remaining coconut milk and peanuts and simmer 10
minutes longer. Serve with garnishes.

CURRIED CHICKEN

Serves 4
2 large onions, sliced
2 cloves garlic, finely chopped
4 tablespoons butter
1/4 teaspoon ground ginger
1 teaspoon ground coriander
1/4 teaspoon ground turmeric
1/8 teaspoon cayenne pepper
1 3-pound fryer chicken, cut up
2 tablespoons plain yogurt
1 bay leaf
1 teaspoon salt
1 tablespoon cornflour, mixed with
3 tablespoons water
accompaniment: freshly cooked rice

In a flameproof casserole brown onions and garlic
in butter; add 1/4 pint water, ginger, coriander, turmeric and cayenne. Stir well and add chicken,
yogurt, bay leaf, salt and 3/4 pint water. Cover and
simmer until tender, about 35 minutes. Just before
serving, blend in cornflour binder and simmer
until sauce is thickened. Serve over rice.

ARROZ CON POLLO, HONDURAN STYLE

Serves 6
1 3-pound fryer chicken, cut up
1 teaspoon salt
4 tablespoons olive oil
1 onion, sliced
1 clove garlic, finely chopped
1 teaspoon caraway seeds
4 tablespoons tomato paste
6 ounces rice
4 ounces pitted black olives
1 pound fresh peas, shelled
scant 1/2 pint light beer
8 ounces shredded cabbage
4 tablespoons capers

Rub chicken pieces with salt. In a large, heavy saucepan or frying pan, brown chicken in hot oil on all sides. Add the onion, garlic, caraway seeds, tomato paste and 3/4 pint water. Bring to a rapid boil, lower heat, cover and simmer 30 minutes. Add remaining ingredients, cover and simmer an additional 30 minutes.

CHICKEN PILAU

Serves 4 to 6
1 3-1/2-pound fryer chicken, cut up
salt and freshly ground pepper to taste
1 onion, chopped
3 celery ribs, chopped
6 to 8 tablespoons raisins
6 tablespoons butter, or
3 tablespoons each butter and corn oil
10 ounces long-grain rice
1/2 pound ripe tomatoes, peeled and chopped
2 tablespoons finely chopped parsley
1 teaspoon dried thyme
1-1/4 pints chicken stock (or half stock and half
  water)
garnish: watercress sprigs

Rub chicken pieces with salt and pepper; set aside. Sauté the onion, celery and raisins in butter in a large frying pan or flameproof casserole until they are soft. Add rice and sauté until rice grains appear translucent; then blend in tomatoes, parsley and thyme. Place chicken pieces on top of rice, add chicken stock and bring to a rapid boil. Lower heat to simmer, cover and cook for 30 minutes, or until chicken is tender and rice has absorbed the liquid. Serve garnished with watercress sprigs.

POULTRY

BRAISED RABBIT WITH POTATOES, ONIONS AND PEAS

Serves 4
1 3-pound rabbit, cut up
2 tablespoons flour
3 tablespoons each butter and olive oil
12 small boiling onions
8 small new potatoes
1 teaspoon salt
1/2 teaspoon freshly ground pepper
1 celery rib, cut up
1 bay leaf
2 cloves garlic
1/2 teaspoon dried thyme
1/2 pint chicken stock
1/4 pint dry white wine
1 pound fresh peas, shelled
garnish: chopped parsley

Top-of-the-Stove Method
(heavy saucepan or flameproof casserole may be used)
Sprinkle the rabbit pieces with flour. Brown rabbit pieces in the butter and oil until golden brown. Add all the remaining ingredients except peas. Bring to a boil, cover and simmer 40 minutes, or until rabbit is tender. Add peas and continue simmering for 10 minutes. Sprinkle with parsley.

Wet Clay Cooker Method
Sprinkle the rabbit pieces with flour. Combine the remaining ingredients, except butter and oil and peas, in a pre-soaked unglazed clay cooker. Place rabbit pieces on top and drizzle with melted butter and oil. Cover and place in a cold oven. Turn oven to 400° and bake 1 hour and 15 minutes. Remove from oven, add peas, cover and bake 10 minutes. Remove from oven and let stand 10 minutes. Garnish with parsley.

CUBAN CHICKEN AND CORN PIE

Serves 6 to 8
3 tablespoons butter
4 eggs, beaten
1 pound fresh or frozen corn kernels, or
1 1-pound can cream-style corn
1/2 pound mild Cheddar cheese, grated
1 pound cooked chicken, diced
2 large carrots, cooked and diced
1 pound fresh peas, shelled
4 to 6 ounces green beans, diagonally sliced
2 ounces pitted black olives, sliced
scant 1/2 pint chicken stock
2 tablespoons raisins
1 small green pepper, diced
1 small red pepper, diced
salt and freshly ground pepper to taste

Butter a 3-pint shallow baking dish with 1 table-spoon of the butter. Combine the eggs, corn and cheese in a bowl. In another bowl, combine all the remaining ingredients except the butter. Layer half the corn mixture in the baking dish and spread vegetable-chicken mixture on top. Top with remaining corn mixture. Dot with the remaining butter and bake in a preheated 350° oven for 1 hour.

STUFFED MELON

Serves 4
1 large cantaloupe melon
3 tablespoons butter
1 onion, chopped
1/2 pound minced chicken or lamb
4 ounces rice or bulgur (cracked wheat), cooked
6 to 8 tablespoons chopped walnuts
6 to 8 tablespoons chopped dried apricots
4 tablespoons honey
1/4 teaspoon ground cinnamon
salt and freshly ground pepper to taste
2 tablespoons sugar

Cut a 1-inch top from melon and reserve for a lid. Discard seeds. Scoop out a cup of melon pulp, chop and reserve. Heat butter in a flameproof casserole and sauté onion until limp. Add meat and brown lightly. Blend in rice or bulgur, nuts, apricots and melon pulp. Mix honey with 1/2 pint hot water and cinnamon. Stir into meat mixture and cook until liquid is absorbed. Season with salt and pepper, remove from heat and cool until lukewarm. Sprinkle inside of melon with sugar, stuff with meat-rice mixture and place in same casserole; replace top and secure with toothpicks. Bake in a preheated 350° oven for 1 hour, or until melon is tender.

POULTRY

PAELLA

Serves 6 to 8

1 2-1/2- to 3-pound fryer chicken,
  cut up, with giblets
salt and freshly ground pepper
6 to 8 tablespoons olive oil
1/2 pound chorizo sausages, blanched and
  cut into 1/2-inch slices
1 small onion, chopped
  cloves garlic, finely chopped
1 red or green pepper, cut into
  1/4-inch wide strips
1-1/4 pounds long grain rice
1/2 pound tomatoes, peeled, seeded and chopped
1/2 teaspoon saffron threads, dissolved in
1/4 pint hot water
1/2 pound medium-sized prawns, shelled and
  deveined with tails intact
12 or more mussels in shells, well scrubbed
4 to 6 ounces fresh peas or asparagus tips, or
  cut-up green beans
garnish: lemon wedges

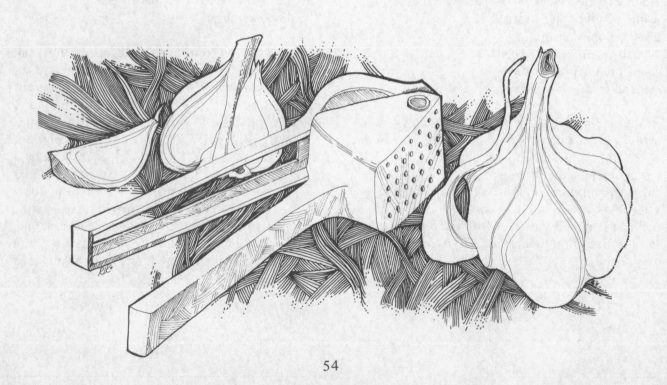

Rub chicken pieces and giblets with salt and pepper. In a large, wide, flameproof casserole, brown the chicken on all sides in half of the olive oil. Remove from pan and set aside. Add chorizo slices to pan, brown and remove. Add remaining oil to pan and sauté onion, garlic, pepper and rice for 5 minutes. Add tomatoes and cook until liquid has evaporated, stirring frequently. Blend in saffron and water and pour 3/4 pint boiling water over all. Cook over high heat until rice has absorbed water. Pour 3/4 pint more boiling water over rice and cook until absorbed. Remove from heat, add chicken pieces and pour 3/4 pint more boiling water over all, placing the prawns, mussels and peas on top. Place pan in a preheated 400° oven for 20 minutes. Adjust seasonings with salt and pepper and serve, garnished with lemon wedges, directly from the pan.

Variations One or more of the following ingredients may be added to paella in substitution for any of the above: lobster, squid, eel, firm fish fillets, rabbit, sweetbreads, veal kidneys, other fowl.

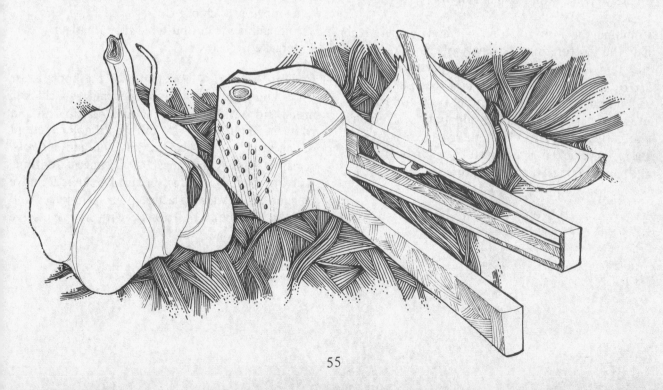

POULTRY

ROAST CHICKEN AND VEGETABLES

Serves 4 to 6
4 tablespoons butter, at room temperature
2 cloves garlic, finely chopped
1 teaspoon salt
1/2 teaspoon freshly ground pepper
1 4-pound roasting chicken
4 sprigs parsley
8 small new potatoes
2 onions, quartered
6 small courgettes, trimmed
2 celery ribs, cut into 2-inch lengths

Combine the butter, garlic, salt and pepper. Rub half the mixture into the cavity of the chicken and the remainder outside. Put the parsley into the cavity and place the chicken in a roasting tin on a rack. Roast in a preheated 400° oven for 15 minutes. Lower heat to 325°, add potatoes, onions, courgettes and celery. Continue roasting for 1 hour. Baste the chicken and vegetables occasionally with the pan drippings. If the pan is too dry, add 1/4 pint water.

ROAST CHICKEN WITH APRICOTS

Serves 4 to 6
4 tablespoons butter, at room temperature
6 tablespoons honey
1 teaspoon rose water or orange flower water
1/2 teaspoon freshly grated nutmeg
1 teaspoon salt
1/2 teaspoon freshly ground pepper
1 4-pound roasting chicken
1 pound fresh apricots, pitted and halved
1 tablespoon sugar
6 to 8 tablespoons toasted silvered almonds or
    chopped pistachios
accompaniment: hot buttered rice or bulgur
    (cracked wheat)

Combine butter, 4 tablespoons of the honey, rose water, nutmeg, salt and pepper and rub chicken inside and out. Place chicken in a roasting tin and roast in a preheated 425° oven until golden, about 45 minutes. Lower heat to 350° and add apricots, remaining honey and sugar to pan juices. Continue roasting for 20 minutes, or until tender. Remove chicken to a warm platter, pour pan juices and apricots over chicken, sprinkle with nuts and serve with rice or bulgur.

ROAST CHICKEN
STUFFED WITH AUBERGINES

Serves 6
1 5-pound roasting chicken
2 tablespoons olive oil
salt and freshly ground pepper to taste
1 aubergine, diced
1 onion, chopped
1 green pepper, diced
2 large tomatoes, peeled and chopped
3 cloves garlic, sliced
1/2 teaspoon dried oregano
1 teaspoon salt
1/2 teaspoon freshly ground pepper

Rub the whole chicken, including cavity, with olive oil; sprinkle inside and out with salt and pepper. Combine the remaining ingredients and stuff the chicken. Truss or sew up opening. Place in a roasting tin in a preheated 325° oven for 1-1/2 to 2 hours, or until chicken is tender. The skin should be nicely browned and crisp. Baste with pan juices occasionally during the roasting period.

Note Pan-browned potatoes may be served with the dish; add as many peeled potatoes as desired to the pan and let bake throughout the roasting period.

POULTRY

TURKEY, CHEESE AND TOMATO OPEN-FACE SANDWICHES

Serves 6
3 tablespoons butter
3 French bread rolls, split
6 slices cooked turkey breast
salt and freshly ground pepper
6 slices mozzarella or mild Cheddar cheese
6 large tomato slices
garnish: chopped basil or parsley

Spread butter on cut side of French rolls. Place a slice of turkey on the cut side of each half. Salt and pepper lightly. Cover each turkey slice with a slice of cheese and a slice of tomato. Place in a shallow baking dish and bake in a preheated 375° oven for 15 minutes, or until cheese has melted. Serve at once, garnished with basil or parsley.

BARLEY CASSEROLE

Serves 4
1/2 pound mushrooms, sliced
1 celery rib, diced
1 onion, diced
4 tablespoons butter
1 pound boneless chicken, diced
7 ounces pearl barley
3/4 pint chicken stock
garnish: chopped parsley

Sauté mushrooms, celery and onion in butter in a saucepan or flameproof casserole until lightly browned; add chicken and barley and continue sautéing for 5 minutes. Add chicken stock and bring to a boil. Lower heat, cover and simmer for 30 minutes. Garnish with parsley.

CHICKEN LIVERS, MIDDLE EASTERN STYLE

Serves 4
1 pound chicken livers, halved
2 tablespoons flour, seasoned with
salt and freshly ground pepper to taste
4 tablespoons olive oil
1 onion, chopped
1 clove garlic, finely chopped
5 ounces bulgur
1/4 teaspoon ground allspice
1/2 pound courgettes, chopped
4 tablespoons currants
2 tablespoons chopped mint
3/4 pint stock
garnish: chopped coriander or parsley

Dredge chicken livers with seasoned flour. In a deep frying pan sauté livers lightly in half the oil. Remove livers to a plate and set aside. In same pan, add remaining oil and sauté onion and garlic until transparent. Add bulgur and continue to sauté until bulgur is shiny, about 2 minutes. Add remaining ingredients and bring to a rapid boil. Lower heat to medium and continue to cook, uncovered, until all liquid is absorbed. Reduce heat to simmer, cover and cook 15 minutes. Place reserved livers on top of bulgur mixture, cover and continue to simmer 5 to 7 minutes to heat through. Serve immediately, garnished with coriander or parsley.

CHICKEN LIVERS PAPRIKA

Serves 4
2 onions, sliced
3 tablespoons corn oil or butter
1 pound chicken livers, halved and sprinkled with
1 tablespoon flour
1 small green pepper, chopped
2 large tomatoes, peeled and chopped
1 tablespoon paprika
salt and freshly ground pepper to taste
scant 1/2 pint sour cream
accompaniment: buttered noodles or freshly
    cooked rice

Sauté the onions in 2 tablespoons of the oil in a frying pan until transparent. Add livers and sauté for 5 minutes; remove onions and livers from the pan and set aside. Add remaining oil to pan; add pepper and tomatoes and cook over medium heat for 10 minutes. Add paprika, salt and pepper. Return chicken livers and onions to pan and cook for 10 minutes. Stir in sour cream and serve over noodles or rice.

LAMB

MEDITERRANEAN LAMB STEW

Serves 6 to 8
2 pounds boneless lamb, cut into 1-inch cubes
6 ounces long-grain rice
1 pound potatoes, peeled and sliced
2 onions, sliced
1 teaspoon salt
1/2 teaspoon freshly ground pepper
1 teaspoon ground cumin
1 pound courgettes, sliced
1 pound fresh peas, shelled, or
1/2 pound green beans, cut in 2-inch lengths
1 pound ripe tomatoes, peeled and diced

Oven Method
Layer about one-third of all ingredients in order listed in a heatproof casserole. Repeat layers twice. Add just enough water to cover. Cover and bake in a preheated 350° oven for 2 hours, or until lamb is tender. Add water if necessary during the cooking. When done, all the water should be absorbed.

Slow Cooker Method
Place sliced potatoes in the bottom of a slow cooker. Layer remaining ingredients on top as directed in oven method. Pour 3/4 pint water over all. Cover and cook on low 8 to 10 hours.

LAMB

IRISH LAMB STEW

Serves 6 to 8

2-1/2 pounds boneless lamb, cut into 1-1/2-inch
   cubes
2 tablespoons corn oil
1-1/2 teaspoons salt
1/2 teaspoon freshly ground pepper
4 turnips, cut into 1/2-inch-thick slices
4 carrots, cut diagonally into 1/2-inch-thick slices
2 onions, sliced
4 potatoes, peeled and quartered
2 tablespoons flour
2 tablespoons chopped parsley

Top-of-the-Stove Method
(flameproof casserole or large saucepan may be used)
Brown lamb on all sides in oil. Sprinkle with salt and pepper. Add 1-1/4 pints water, bring to boil, reduce heat and simmer, covered, for 1 hour. Add vegetables to pot and bring to a boil again; reduce heat and simmer, covered, for 30 minutes, or until meat and vegetables are tender. Blend the flour smoothly with 4 tablespoons water; slowly add to the stew, stirring constantly until slightly thickened. Stir in parsley and serve.

Slow Cooker Method
Brown meat in oil in a frying pan or a slow cooker with a browning unit. Put all ingredients except flour and parsley in a slow cooker with the meat. Add 3/4 pint water; cook on low, covered, for 8 to 10 hours. Uncover and turn on high. Blend the flour smoothly with 4 tablespoons water; slowly add to the stew, stirring constantly until slightly thickened. Stir in parsley and serve.

Pressure Cooker Method

Brown meat in oil in a pressure cooker. Add 1-1/4 pints water, cover and bring to full pressure. When steam appears, reduce heat and cook on low 15 minutes. Reduce pressure completely, add salt, pepper, turnips, carrots, onions and potatoes, cover and simmer, not under pressure, 30 minutes. Blend the flour smoothly with 4 tablespoons water; slowly add to the stew, stirring constantly until slightly thickened. Stir in parsley and serve.

Wet Clay Cooker Method

Combine all ingredients except flour and parsley, in a pre-soaked unglazed clay cooker. Add 3/4 pint water, cover and place in a cold oven. Turn oven to 400° and bake 1-1/2 hours. Remove from oven. Blend the flour smoothly with 4 tablespoons water; slowly add to the stew, stirring constantly until slightly thickened. Cover and let stand 10 minutes. Stir in parsley and serve.

LAMB AND OKRA STEW

Serves 6 to 8

2 pounds boneless lamb, cut into 1-inch cubes
2 tablespoons corn oil
1 onion, chopped
2 tablespoons flour
1 6-ounce can tomato paste
1 green pepper, cut into strips
1 teaspoon salt
1/2 teaspoon freshly ground pepper
1 pound okra, cut into 1/2-inch-thick slices
accompaniment: freshly cooked rice or
    French bread

Brown lamb in oil in a saucepan. Add onion and flour and brown. Add tomato paste, pepper strips, salt, pepper and 1-1/4 pints water. Simmer covered for 1-1/2 hours. Add okra and cook until just tender. Serve with freshly cooked rice or French bread.

LAMB

STUFFED LEG OF LAMB

Serves 6 to 8

1 5-pound leg of lamb, boned
1 teaspoon salt
1 teaspoon freshly ground pepper
4 tablespoons raisins
4 tablespoons chopped pitted dates
4 tablespoons each chopped dried figs and dried
 apricots
4 tablespoons pine nuts
1 small onion, chopped
4 ounces bulgur, soaked in water to cover
 15 minutes and drained
2 tablespoons chopped parsley or coriander
accompaniment: spinach salad with vinaigrette
 dressing

Rub leg of lamb with salt and pepper. Combine all
the remaining ingredients and stuff lamb with mixture; fasten with skewers. Roast on a rack in a
roasting tin in a preheated 325° oven for about 2
hours or until done. Baste occasionally with pan
juices. Serve with a spinach salad with vinaigrette
dressing, if desired.

BOILED LEG OF LAMB

Serves 8

3 cloves garlic, cut in slivers
1 6-pound leg of lamb
6 peppercorns
2 bay leaves
2 sprigs parsley
1 tablespoon salt
4 celery ribs, cut into 4-inch lengths with
 some leaves
8 carrots, halved
4 turnips, halved
8 small onions
1 medium-sized cabbage, cut in 8 wedges
8 new potatoes

Insert garlic slivers with a sharply pointed, narrow
knife into various parts of leg. Wrap leg in 2 thick-
nesses of cheesecloth and tie with white string.
Place the lamb in a large pot and cover with cold
water. Bring to a boil, skimming off any surface
scum, and add peppercorns, bay leaves, parsley and
salt. Lower heat, cover and simmer 45 minutes.
Add remaining vegetables and cover and simmer 45
minutes longer. Remove leg of lamb from pot and
unwrap it; place on warm platter. Remove vegetables from broth and surround lamb with them.
Strain broth and serve in cups.

STUFFED CROWN ROAST OF LAMB

Serves 8
1 5- to 6-pound crown roast of lamb
1 pound minced lamb
1 onion, chopped
1 tablespoon olive oil
1 teaspoon salt
1/2 teaspoon freshly ground pepper
1/4 teaspoon each ground cinnamon, cardamom,
    ginger and cloves
5 to 6 ounces rice or bulgur (cracked wheat),
    cooked
6 to 8 tablespoons raisins
6 to 8 tablespoons chopped toasted almonds
garnish:
    watercress sprigs
    orange slices

Have butcher prepare crown roast for stuffing. In a frying pan brown the lamb and onion in oil about 5 minutes. Remove from heat and combine with spices, rice, raisins and almonds and stuff crown roast with this mixture. Place roast in a roasting tin, cover top of roast and stuffing with foil and roast in preheated 325° oven for 2 hours or until lamb is done. Remove foil during last 15 minutes of roasting to brown top. Garnish with watercress and orange slices and serve.

LEG OF LAMB WITH HERBS AND VEGETABLES

Serves 6
1 4- to 5-pound leg of lamb
4 tablespoons finely chopped parsley
2 cloves garlic, finely chopped
1/2 teaspoon dried marjoram
2 sprigs rosemary, chopped, or
1/2 teaspoon dried rosemary
1/4 pound Parma ham, cut into 1/2-inch-wide strips
salt and freshly ground pepper to taste
4 tablespoons olive oil
generous 1/2 pint dry white wine
3 or 4 carrots, halved
6 to 8 new potatoes
6 to 8 small boiling onions

Wipe meat with a damp cloth and make several slashes over the surface. Mix together parsley, garlic, marjoram and rosemary and brush mixture over ham strips. Force ham strips into slashes in lamb leg. Rub the lamb with salt and pepper and any remaining herb mixture. Brown the lamb in oil in a flameproof casserole. When browned, add wine and vegetables. Cover and simmer for 40 minutes or until tender, basting occasionally with pan juices and adding a little water if needed.

COURGETTES STUFFED WITH LAMB AND PINE NUTS

Serves 6 to 8
8 medium-sized courgettes
1 tablespoon olive oil
6 to 8 tablespoons pine nuts
4 tablespoons butter
1 pound minced lamb or veal
1 medium-sized onion, chopped
pinch of dried rosemary
1 teaspoon salt
1/8 teaspoon freshly ground pepper
accompaniment: 3/4 pint plain yogurt

Wash and core courgettes, leaving whole. Rub with oil. In a large frying pan, sauté pine nuts in 2 tablespoons of the butter until golden; remove from pan and set aside. In the same pan, melt remaining butter and brown meat and onion. Combine meat, nuts, and seasonings. Cool mixture and stuff cored courgettes with meat mixture. Place stuffed courgettes in pan; add 1/4 pint water, cover and simmer for 20 minutes, or until courgettes are tender. Serve with yogurt.

STUFFED COURGETTES
WITH LAMB AND BULGUR

Serves 6

12 medium-sized courgettes
1 pound minced lamb
5 ounces bulgur (cracked wheat), soaked in water
    to cover 15 minutes and drained
1 teaspoon salt
1/2 teaspoon ground allspice
1 6-ounce can tomato paste
2 tablespoons olive oil
2 cloves garlic, finely chopped
2 tablespoons fresh lemon juice

Cut courgettes in half lengthwise and scoop out
centers. Dice pulp and add lamb, bulgur, salt and
allspice. Mix well and fill courgette halves with this
stuffing. Place courgettes in one layer in a buttered
baking dish. Combine tomato paste, olive oil, garlic
and lemon juice and spread over courgettes. Add
3/4 pint water to pan. Cover with aluminium foil
and bake in a preheated 350° oven for 45 minutes.

LAMB

LAMB RISOTTO

Serves 6
4 tablespoons butter
1 medium-sized onion, sliced
1-1/2 pounds boneless lamb, cut into 1-inch cubes
1 pound ripe tomatoes, peeled, seeded and chopped
salt and freshly ground pepper to taste
pinch of ground cinnamon
1 pound long-grain rice
1-1/4 pints each lamb or chicken stock and water, heated
3 ounces Parmesan cheese, grated

Melt butter in a flameproof casserole and sauté onion until brown. Add meat and brown on all sides. Add tomatoes, salt, pepper and cinnamon. Cover and simmer 1 hour. Raise heat and add rice with 1 cup of the stock. Cook uncovered for 5 minutes or until the rice has absorbed the stock. Add remaining stock, cup by cup, until all the stock has been absorbed. Sprinkle with Parmesan and serve immediately.

MIXED MEATLOAF WITH APPLES AND PRUNES

Serves 8 to 10
1 pound minced lamb
1 pound minced pork
1 pound minced veal
1 onion, chopped
1 tablespoon salt
1/2 teaspoon freshly ground pepper
1/2 teaspoon ground allspice
6 to 8 tablespoons bread crumbs
6 to 8 tablespoons milk
6 ounces dried sliced apples, plumped in 1/2 pint warm water
6 ounces dried pitted prunes, plumped in 1/2 pint warm water

Combine meats, onion, seasonings, bread crumbs and milk. Place half of the meat mixture in a buttered, 5-pint, ovenproof casserole. Drain dried fruits, reserving soaking water, and place fruit on top of meat mixture. Top with remaining meat mixture. Pack firmly. Pour soaking water over all. Cover and bake in a preheated 350° oven for 1-1/2 hours.

MOUSSAKA

Serves 6

2 aubergines, peeled, sliced 1/2 inch thick, salted, drained and dried on paper toweling
flour
corn oil as needed
1 onion, finely chopped
1 pound minced lamb
5 tablespoons butter
2 tablespoons tomato paste
6 to 8 tablespoons finely chopped parsley
4 tablespoons dry red wine
freshly ground pepper
1/4 teaspoon ground cinnamon
1 egg, beaten
4 tablespoons bread crumbs
3/4 pint White Sauce, page 41
2 egg yolks, slightly beaten
freshly grated nutmeg
6 to 8 tablespoons grated Parmesan cheese

Sprinkle aubergine slices lightly with flour. In a frying pan, fry slices in oil until golden. Remove from the pan and set aside. Pour off oil, return pan to the heat and sauté onion and lamb in butter; add tomato paste, parsley, wine, pepper, cinnamon and egg and mix well. Sprinkle half the bread crumbs in a buttered 3-pint baking dish. Top with a layer of aubergine slices and meat mixture; repeat layers until all ingredients have been used, finishing with a layer of aubergine. Make White Sauce, beating in egg yolks and nutmeg at last minute; pour over top of moussaka, sprinkle with remaining bread crumbs and the Parmesan cheese. Bake in a preheated 350° oven for 1 hour or until top is golden.

LAMB

LAMB BAKED WITH TOMATOES AND POTATOES

Serves 6
1 large onion, sliced
2 tablespoons each olive oil and butter
2 pounds boneless lamb, cut into 1-inch cubes
2 sprigs rosemary, chopped, or
1/2 teaspoon dried rosemary
1/4 pint dry white wine
1 teaspoon salt
1/2 teaspoon freshly ground pepper
1 pound ripe tomatoes, peeled, seeded and chopped
1-1/2 pounds new potatoes

Oven Method
In a 3-pint flameproof casserole sauté onion in olive oil and butter until transparent; add lamb and rosemary and brown meat on all sides. Add wine and simmer until wine evaporates. Sprinkle with salt and pepper. Add tomatoes and potatoes and place casserole in a preheated 375° oven. Bake, covered, for 1 hour.

Slow Cooker Method
Sauté onion in olive oil and butter until transparent in a frying pan or slow cooker with browning unit. Add lamb and rosemary and brown meat on all sides. Cut potatoes into quarters, place in bottom of a slow cooker and top with all remaining ingredients. Cook, covered, on low 6 to 8 hours.

LAMB CURRY

Serves 6
3 cloves garlic
1 tablespoon grated ginger root
2 whole cloves
1 2-inch piece cinnamon stick
3 cardamom pods, peeled
1 teaspoon ground coriander
2 to 4 dried red chili peppers, seeded
1/2 teaspoon salt
2 tablespoons brown sugar
1/2 pint coconut milk, page 20
2 pounds boneless lamb, cut into 1-inch cubes
3 tablespoons each butter and corn oil
4 large onions, thinly sliced
1 tart apple, peeled and chopped
freshly cooked rice

suggested accompaniments: chutney, raisins, chopped, roasted or fried cashews, grated coconut, sliced bananas, chopped green pepper, chopped cucumber, chopped spring onions, chopped coriander, hard-boiled eggs with whites and yolks chopped separately

Purée garlic, spices, sugar and coconut milk in a blender and marinate lamb in this mixture for 2 or more hours. Heat butter and oil in a large frying pan. Sauté onions until transparent. Lower heat, add lamb, marinade and apple and simmer for 30 minutes or until lamb is tender. Serve over a bed of hot rice with as many of the condiments as desired.

LAMB

MUSTARD COATED LAMB

Serves 2 or 3
4 tablespoons toasted sesame seeds
12 small salty crackers
Dijon-style mustard
6 slices cooked lamb, sliced 1/4 inch thick
2 tablespoons each butter and corn oil
6 slices pumpernickel bread
garnish:
    watercress sprigs
    tomato slices

Combine the sesame seeds and crackers in a blender to make fine crumbs, and transfer to a plate. Spread mustard on both sides of the lamb slices and roll slices in crumbs. Sauté in butter and oil in a frying pan until lamb is lightly browned on both sides. Place lamb slices on bread. Garnish with watercress and tomato slices.

Variations Cooked turkey, roast beef or roast pork slices may be substituted for the lamb.

LAMB CHOPS WITH GREEN BEANS

Serves 6 to 8
2 pounds lamb chops, cut 3/4 inch thick
1 clove garlic, finely chopped
1 onion, chopped
1/2 teaspoon dried marjoram
3 tablespoons olive oil
salt and freshly ground pepper to taste
1/2 pint dry white wine
1 tablespoon tomato paste
1/2 pound green beans, cut in 2-inch lengths
accompaniment:
    boiled new potatoes
    chopped parsley

In a large frying pan, brown lamb with garlic, onion and marjoram in oil. Season with salt and pepper, add wine and cook over medium heat until wine evaporates. Mix tomato paste with 1/2 pint water and add to pan. Add green beans, cover and simmer for 30 minutes. Remove to a warm platter and serve, surrounded by new potatoes sprinkled with chopped parsley.

SAFFRON RICE WITH SPICY LAMB

Serves 8
3/4 pound long-grain rice, washed and drained
1/4 teaspoon saffron threads, soaked in
4 tablespoons hot water
2 onions, sliced
1/4 pound butter (or half butter and half
   corn oil)
4 tablespoons unsalted cashews
4 tablespoons slivered blanched almonds
5 tablespoons raisins
1 tablespoon finely chopped ginger root
2 cloves garlic, finely chopped
1/2 teaspoon ground cumin
2 pounds boneless lamb, cut into 1-inch cubes
1 stick cinnamon
1/4 teaspoon powdered cloves
1/4 teaspoon cayenne pepper
1/4 teaspoon ground cardamom
1/4 teaspoon freshly grated nutmeg
generous 1/2 pint chicken stock
8 fluid ounces plain yogurt
salt and freshly ground pepper to taste

In a flameproof casserole or in a large saucepan, bring 3 pints water to boil. Add rice, lower heat and simmer covered for 10 minutes; drain and set aside, covering with saffron water. Sauté onions in half of the butter until golden. With a slotted spoon remove onions to a plate. Sauté nuts in same pan, adding more butter if needed. With a slotted spoon remove nuts to a plate and set aside. Repeat procedure with raisins. Add remaining butter to pan and cook ginger root, garlic and cumin 1 minute. Add meat, browning on all sides. Blend in remaining spices, half the stock and the yogurt. Cover and simmer 20 minutes. Spoon reserved rice evenly over lamb mixture and sprinkle remaining stock over rice. Cover again and simmer for 15 minutes. Serve lamb and rice on a large platter, with cinnamon stick removed, and reserved onions, nuts and raisins sprinkled on top.

PORK

PORK MEATBALLS WITH POTATOES

Serves 3 or 4

1 pound lean minced pork
1/8 teaspoon freshly grated nutmeg
1/2 teaspoon salt
1/2 teaspoon freshly ground pepper
3 ounces fresh bread crumbs
1 egg, beaten
4 tablespoons corn oil
3 tablespoons butter
2 tablespoons finely chopped shallots
1 clove garlic, finely chopped
2 onions, sliced
4 potatoes, peeled and quartered
1/4 pint dry white wine
1/2 pint chicken stock
garnish: chopped parsley

Combine the pork, nutmeg, salt, pepper, bread crumbs and egg. Form into meatballs, each about the size of a large egg. Heat oil in a frying pan and brown the meatballs on all sides. Remove to a plate. Pour off excess oil remaining in the pan, add butter and sauté shallots, garlic and onions for 2 minutes. Return meatballs to the pan, surround with potatoes and pour wine and stock over all. Bring to a boil, lower heat, cover and simmer for 25 minutes or until the potatoes are tender. Sprinkle with parsley and serve.

PORK

BIGOS

Serves 6

1 onion, chopped
1 clove garlic, finely chopped
2 tablespoons butter or lard
1 pound cabbage, shredded
1 pound sauerkraut, rinsed and drained
1/4 pound mushrooms, sliced
1 pound boneless pork, cut into 1-inch cubes
1 pound boneless veal, cut into 1-inch cubes
1/2 pound Polish sausage, sliced 1/2 inch thick
1/2 pint beef stock
1/2 pound ripe tomatoes, peeled and chopped
2 tart apples, peeled and diced
3 ounces pitted prunes
1 bay leaf
1 teaspoon salt
1/2 teaspoon freshly ground pepper
1/2 pint red wine

Top-of-the-Stove Method
In a large pan, sauté onion and garlic in butter until onion is transparent. Add remaining ingredients, cover and simmer for 2 hours.

Slow Cooker Method
Combine all the ingredients, reducing stock and wine to 1/4 pint each, and cook on low, covered, 8 to 10 hours.

Pressure Cooker Method
In a pressure cooker sauté the onion and garlic in butter until onion is transparent. Combine the remaining ingredients, adding 1/2 pint water, and cover and bring to full pressure. When steam appears, reduce heat and cook on low 30 minutes. Reduce pressure completely and let stand 10 to 15 minutes to blend flavors.

Wet Clay Cooker Method
Combine all ingredients in a pre-soaked unglazed clay cooker, cover and place in a cold oven. Turn oven to 400° and bake 1-1/2 hours. Remove from oven and let rest 15 minutes before serving.

SZEKELY GULYAS
(Pork and Sauerkraut Stew)

Serves 6
2 onions, chopped
2 tablespoons lard
2 cloves garlic, finely chopped
1 teaspoon caraway seeds
2 tablespoons paprika
2 pounds boneless pork, cut into 1-inch cubes
1 teaspoon salt
3/4 pound sauerkraut, rinsed and drained
1 tablespoon flour
3/4 pint sour cream
accompaniment: buttered noodles

Top-of-the-Stove Method
(heavy saucepan or large frying pan may be used)
Sauté onions in lard until they become transparent; then add garlic, caraway seeds, paprika and 1/2 pint water. Bring to a boil and add meat and salt. Lower heat, cover and simmer for 1 hour. Add sauerkraut and continue cooking for 25 minutes. Mix the flour with the sour cream and add to the stew, simmering for 5 minutes. Serve with buttered noodles.

Slow Cooker Method
Combine all ingredients, except flour and sour cream, adding 1/4 pint water. Cook on low, covered, for 8 to 10 hours. Uncover and turn on high. Mix the flour with the sour cream, add to the stew and continue cooking for 5 to 10 minutes to heat through. Serve with buttered noodles.

Pressure Cooker Method
In a pressure cooker sauté onions in lard until they become transparent. Then add remaining ingredients except sauerkraut, flour and sour cream. Add 1/2 pint water. Cover and bring to full pressure. When steam appears, reduce heat and cook on low 20 minutes. Reduce pressure completely, uncover and add sauerkraut. Cover and cook for 25 minutes, not under pressure. Mix the flour with the sour cream and add to the stew, simmering for 5 minutes. Serve with buttered noodles.

PORK

PORK, SAUERKRAUT
AND BARLEY CASSEROLE

Serves 6
1 3-pound pork loin roast
1-1/2 pounds sauerkraut, rinsed and drained
1 onion, thinly sliced
6 to 8 tablespoons pearl barley, rinsed and drained
2 bay leaves
1/2 teaspoon freshly ground pepper

Oven Method
Place pork in a large, ovenproof casserole. Top with sauerkraut and onion. Sprinkle barley over sauerkraut. Tuck in bay leaves and grind pepper over top. Pour water to the top of the sauerkraut (about 1-1/2 pints) and cover. Bake in a preheated 350° oven for 3 hours. Remove pork, slice and serve with sauerkraut-barley mixture.

Slow Cooker Method
Place ingredients in slow cooker as directed in oven method, reducing water to 3/4 pint. Cook on low, covered, 10 to 12 hours. Serve as directed in oven method.

ROAST LOIN OF PORK
WITH POTATOES AND APPLES

Serves 6
1 5- to 6-pound loin of pork with some fat on it
salt and freshly ground pepper to taste
pinch of ground allspice
6 medium-sized onions
6 medium-sized potatoes, peeled
6 baking apples, cored
1 to 2 teaspoons cornflour
generous 1/2 pint dry cider
4 to 6 tablespoons Calvados (optional)

Rub the loin of pork with salt, pepper and allspice and place in a roasting tin. Surround with onions and potatoes and roast, covered, in a preheated 325° oven for 1-1/2 to 2 hours. Uncover, add apples and continue roasting 1 hour longer to brown meat. Allow 35 minutes per pound of meat; meat thermometer will read 170° when roast is done. Turn potatoes and onions during cooking. Remove meat to a warm platter and surround with potatoes, onions and apples. Pour off excess fat from the tin. Mix cornflour with the cider and Calvados. Add to the tin and stir over high heat on stovetop, until sauce begins to thicken. Simmer 5 minutes. Slice roast and pour sauce over slices to serve.

CALIFORNIA HASH

Serves 4 to 6
3/4 pound lean minced pork
3/4 pound lean minced beef
1 teaspoon salt
1/2 teaspoon freshly ground pepper
6 to 8 tablespoons dry sherry
1 onion, chopped
2 cloves garlic, finely chopped
1 green pepper, chopped
3 tablespoons capers
2 ounces pitted green olives, sliced
3 tablespoons olive oil
1 bay leaf
1/4 teaspoon ground cumin
1/2 teaspoon dried oregano
6 to 8 tablespoons puréed fresh or canned
    tomatoes
6 to 8 tablespoons raisins
6 to 8 tablespoons slivered blanched almonds
accompaniment: French bread

Combine the meats, salt, pepper and sherry and let stand for 1 hour. In a frying pan sauté onion, garlic, green pepper, capers and olives in oil. Blend in the meat mixture, bay leaf, cumin, oregano, tomato purée, raisins and almonds. Cover and cook over low heat for 40 minutes. Serve with warm French bread.

PORK

HUNGARIAN CABBAGE ROLLS

Serves 6 to 8
1 large head cabbage
3/4 pound minced pork
3/4 pound minced beef
1 small onion, chopped
6 ounces rice
1 egg, beaten
1 tablespoon salt
1/2 teaspoon freshly ground pepper
1 tablespoon paprika
1/2 pound sauerkraut, rinsed and drained
3/4 pint each tomato juice and water
8 fluid ounces sour cream

Top-of-the-Stove Method
(large saucepan or flameproof casserole may be used)
Remove core from cabbage, place in a large bowl and pour boiling water over to cover. Let stand until the cabbage has wilted, about 5 minutes. Drain and remove the leaves, leaving them whole. Trim off the heavy stem and flatten the leaves. Combine the meats, onion, rice, egg, salt, pepper and paprika. Put about 2 tablespoons of this mixture on each cabbage leaf, fold sides in like an envelope and roll up. Place rolls seam side down in pot. Spread the sauerkraut on top of the rolls and add tomato juice and water. Bring to a boil, reduce heat, cover and simmer for 1-1/2 hours. Carefully lift the cabbage rolls out onto a warm platter. Blend 1/4 pint of the broth from the pot with the sour cream and pour over the cabbage rolls.

Slow Cooker Method
Proceed with recipe as for top-of-the-stove method, reducing tomato juice and water by a quarter. Cook on low, covered, for 6 to 8 hours. Remove cabbage rolls and complete recipe as directed for top-of-the-stove method.

Pressure Cooker Method
Proceed with recipe as for top-of-the-stove method. Cover and bring to full pressure. When steam appears, reduce heat and cook on low for 20 minutes. Reduce pressure completely and let stand covered 10 to 15 minutes to blend flavors. Lift out cabbage rolls and complete recipe as directed for top-of-the-stove method.

STUFFED WHOLE CABBAGE

Serves 6 to 8
1 large curly Savoy cabbage
1/2 pound pork sausage meat
1-1/2 pounds minced veal
1/4 pound mushrooms, chopped
1 onion, chopped
2 cloves garlic, finely chopped
1 teaspoon salt
1/2 teaspoon freshly ground pepper
2 tablespoons butter or olive oil
2 onions, quartered
4 carrots, sliced
2 turnips, sliced
3/4 pint beef stock or water
1 bay leaf
1/2 teaspoon dried thyme
1 pound fresh peas, shelled
accompaniment: French bread

Top-of-the-Stove Method
Place cabbage in a large bowl and pour boiling water over to cover. Let stand 5 minutes or until limp. Combine meats, mushrooms, chopped onion, garlic, salt and pepper and stuff mixture between all leaves except the two outer leaves. Tie cabbage firmly with string, pressing back into original shape. Place cabbage in a large soup pot. Surround with remaining ingredients, except peas. Cover, bring to a boil, reduce heat and simmer for 1-1/2 hours or until cabbage is cooked through. Add peas for last 5 minutes of cooking time. To serve, cut cabbage into wedges and serve with vegetables. Strain broth and serve in cups, accompanied by French bread.

Slow Cooker Method
Prepare cabbage as directed for top-of-the-stove method and place in slow cooker with all remaining ingredients, except peas. Cook on low, covered, for 6 to 8 hours. Add peas, cover and cook on high for 15 minutes.

Pressure Cooker Method
Prepare cabbage as directed for top-of-the-stove method. Place in pressure cooker with all remaining ingredients, except peas, increasing stock to 1-1/4 pints and cutting vegetables in chunks rather than slices. Cover and bring to full pressure. When steam appears, reduce heat and cook on low for 20 minutes. Reduce pressure completely, uncover and add peas. Cover and continue cooking for 5 minutes, not under pressure. Let stand, covered, for 10 to 15 minutes to blend flavors.

PORK

RICE WITH ITALIAN SAUSAGE AND COURGETTES

Serves 4

1/2 pound Italian sausages, sliced 1/2 inch thick
1 onion, chopped
2 tablespoons each butter and olive oil
1 pound courgettes, sliced 1/4 inch thick
6 to 8 tablespoons dry white wine
about 1-1/2 pints chicken stock
6 ounces rice
3 sprigs parsley, finely chopped
3 ounces Parmesan cheese, grated

In a frying pan sauté sausages and onion in butter and oil until sausages are browned. Add courgettes and sauté for 2 minutes. Pour in wine and cook until evaporated. Add stock and bring to a boil. Add rice, reduce heat to low and cook until rice is tender, about 20 minutes. When rice has thoroughly absorbed stock, stir in parsley and Parmesan and serve immediately.

STUFFED LETTUCE, PARISIAN STYLE

Serves 4

8 large lettuce leaves, Cos or Webb's Wonderful
1 pound pork sausage meat
1 teaspoon dried marjoram
2 tablespoons chopped chives
2 tablespoons chopped parsley
1 small green pepper, chopped
1 slice bread, trimmed and crumbled
1 egg, beaten
6 to 8 tablespoons milk
generous 1/4 pint tomato juice
3 tablespoons butter
accompaniment: French bread

Pour boiling water over the lettuce leaves and let stand for 2 minutes, or until just limp. Drain and pat leaves dry. Combine the remaining ingredients except the tomato sauce and butter. Divide filling mixture into 8 portions and place each on a lettuce leaf. Fold sides in like an envelope and roll up. Place seam side down in a buttered baking dish. Pour tomato sauce over the stuffed leaves. Dot with butter. Cover with foil and bake in a preheated 350° oven for 40 minutes. Remove foil and bake 10 minutes longer to brown top lightly. Serve with French bread.

Variations Substitute any minced raw or cooked meat, fish or poultry for the pork sausage.

STUFFED AUBERGINES, CREOLE STYLE

Serves 4
2 aubergines, about 1 pound each
4 tablespoons olive oil
3 tablespoons butter
1 small onion, chopped
2 spring onions, chopped
2 cloves garlic, finely chopped
1/2 pound ripe tomatoes, peeled and chopped
1/2 teaspoon dried thyme
1/4 teaspoon cayenne pepper
1/2 teaspoon freshly ground pepper
1/2 pound cooked ham, minced
3 ounces fresh French bread crumbs
2 tablespoons chopped coriander or parsley

Cut the aubergines in half lengthwise and remove pulp to make a scooped-out shell, 1/2 inch thick. Chop the aubergine pulp and set aside. Heat the olive oil in a large frying pan and gently cook aubergine shells, cut side down, for 5 minutes. Turn shells over, cover and cook 5 minutes longer. Remove shells to a shallow baking dish. Add butter to pan, with any remaining oil, and sauté onions and garlic for 2 minutes. Add reserved aubergine pulp, tomatoes, thyme, cayenne and pepper and cook over brisk heat until most of the liquid has evaporated and the mixture is thick. Remove from heat and mix in ham, bread crumbs and coriander. Fill the aubergine shells and bake in a preheated 400° oven for 15 minutes or until slightly browned.

SCALLOPED POTATOES AND HAM

Serves 4
1/2 pound cooked ham, diced
2 pounds potatoes, peeled and thinly sliced
3/4 pint milk
1/2 teaspoon dry mustard
1 small onion, grated
3 tablespoons butter

Butter the bottom and sides of a 3-pint baking dish. Beginning with the ham, alternate layers of ham and potatoes, finishing with a layer of potatoes. Combine the milk, mustard and onion, and pour over all. Dot with butter. Cover and bake in a preheated 325° oven for 1 hour or until potatoes are tender. Remove cover and continue cooking for 15 minutes or until browned.

PORK

BAKED HAM
WITH MADEIRA AND RAISIN SAUCE
(Served with Baked Sweet Potatoes)

Serves 10 or more
4 ounces raisins
generous 1/2 pint Madeira
1 10-pound precooked smoked ham
scant 1/2 pint beef stock
1 onion, stuck with 2 cloves
1 bay leaf
1 teaspoon cornflour, dissolved in
1 tablespoon water
5 orange slices, halved
1 tablespoon butter
garnish: watercress sprigs

Soak raisins in Madeira overnight. Remove skin from ham, leaving a 1/4-inch layer of fat. Put the ham in a roasting tin. Drain raisins, reserving Madeira, and set aside. Add the Madeira, stock, onion and bay leaf to the tin. Cover and bake in a preheated 350° oven for 1-1/2 hours. Baste every 20 minutes during cooking. Transfer the ham to a warm platter, remove onion and bay leaf from the pan and skim off as much fat as possible. Place the tin over high heat on stovetop and reduce juices to a generous 1/2 pint. Thicken with cornflour. Add the reserved raisins and orange slices and simmer for 5 minutes. Stir in the butter until melted. Slice ham and garnish with the orange slices and watercress. Pour 1/4 pint sauce over the ham and serve remaining sauce on the side.

Baked Sweet Potatoes
Scrub sweet potatoes, 1 per serving. Place on rack in a preheated 350° oven (these can bake on the rack above the ham) for 1 hour or more, depending on the size of the sweet potatoes, until tender. Serve with butter and a pinch of freshly grated nutmeg.

SCHNITZ UND KNEPPE

Serves 6 to 8
1 3-pound smoked ham with bone
3/4 pound dried apples
1 tablespoon brown sugar

Dumplings
6 ounces unbleached white flour
1 tablespoon baking powder
1/2 teaspoon salt
1 ounce butter
3 to 4 tablespoons milk
1 egg, well beaten

In a large pan or flameproof casserole, cover ham with cold water and bring to a rapid boil. Skim any surface scum. Lower heat, cover and simmer for 1 hour. While ham is cooking, soak apples in water for 1 hour and drain. Add apples and brown sugar to pot and continue simmering for 1 hour. Remove ham to platter and surround with apples; keep warm. Reserve ham broth to make dumplings.

To make dumplings, sift together the flour, baking powder and salt. Cut butter into flour mixture with 2 knives or a pastry blender. Combine the milk and egg and add to the flour and butter mixture, mixing well. Bring ham broth to a boil and drop in dumplings from a soup spoon. Cover tightly and simmer 10 to 12 minutes. Lift dumplings out with a slotted spoon and arrange on the platter with the ham and apples. Spoon a little ham broth over all.

MEAT-AND-SPINACH ROLLS

Serves 4
3/4 pound spinach, cooked and chopped
2 hard-boiled eggs, chopped
2 tablespoons butter, melted
salt and freshly ground pepper to taste
pinch of freshly grated nutmeg
12 thin slices cooked meat, such as ham,
   beef, lamb or tongue
8 ounces wide egg noodles, cooked al dente and
   tossed lightly with butter
1 tablespoon prepared horseradish
1 teaspoon Dijon-style mustard
generous 1/4 pint double cream

Combine spinach, eggs, butter, salt, pepper and nutmeg. Place a spoonful of the mixture on each slice of meat and roll up, fastening with toothpicks. Layer bottom of buttered baking dish with cooked noodles. Place rolls on top. Combine remaining ingredients and pour over all. Bake in a preheated 400° oven for 20 minutes or until heated through.

BEEF

OVEN POT ROAST WITH ONION GRAVY

Serves 6 to 8
1 4-pound beef pot roast
1/2 teaspoon ground cinnamon
1/2 teaspoon freshly grated nutmeg
1 teaspoon dry mustard
1 teaspoon salt
1/2 teaspoon freshly ground pepper
4 large onions, sliced
3/4 pint beef stock
accompaniments:
   freshly cooked noodles
   sliced tomatoes and cucumbers

Rub the meat with a mixture of the cinnamon, nutmeg, mustard, salt and pepper. Place meat in a roasting tin, surround with onions and pour in stock. Cover and bake in a preheated 300° oven for 3 hours. Slice and serve with freshly cooked noodles and sliced tomatoes and cucumbers.

Variations
• Add 4 ounces mushrooms to the roast for the last hour of cooking.
• Add 12 ounces fresh peas for the last 30 minutes of cooking.
• Blend 1/2 pint sour cream into the pan juices and heat through before serving.

BEEF

BEEF BOURGUIGNON

Serves 6

1/4 pound salt pork, well rinsed and cut into
    1/2-inch dice
2 pounds lean boneless beef, cut into 1-inch cubes
scant 1/2 pint beef stock
scant 1/2 pint Burgundy
2 sprigs parsley
1/4 teaspoon dried thyme
1 bay leaf
1 carrot, grated
1/2 teaspoon freshly ground pepper
2 tablespoons butter
6 to 8 small boiling onions
1/2 pound small button mushrooms
1 pound fresh peas, shelled
garnish: chopped parsley
accompaniment: freshly cooked rice

Top-of-the-Stove Method

Sauté salt pork in a flameproof casserole until fat runs; do not brown. Remove pork with a slotted spoon and add beef, browning on all sides. Add reserved salt pork, stock, Burgundy, parsley, thyme, bay leaf, carrot and pepper. Bring just to a boil, cover, lower heat and simmer for 1 to 1-1/2 hours or until meat is tender. Add butter, onions and mushrooms and continue cooking, covered, for 15 minutes. Add peas and cook 5 minutes. Serve, garnished with parsley, over rice.

Slow Cooker Method

Sauté salt pork in a frying pan or slow cooker with browning unit until fat is rendered; do not brown. Remove salt pork with a slotted spoon and add beef, browning on all sides. Combine browned meat, reserved salt pork, only 1/4 pint each beef stock and Burgundy, parsley, thyme, bay leaf, carrot, pepper and onions in a slow cooker. Cover and cook on low 6 to 8 hours. Add butter, mushrooms and peas and cook on high 15 minutes. Serve, garnished with parsley, over rice.

Pressure Cooker Method
In a pressure cooker sauté salt pork until fat is rendered; do not brown. Remove salt pork with a slotted spoon and add beef, browning on all sides. Add reserved salt pork, stock, Burgundy, parsley, thyme, bay leaf, carrot, pepper and 1/2 pint water. Cover and bring to full pressure. When steam appears, reduce heat and cook on low 20 minutes. Reduce pressure completely, uncover and add butter, onions and mushrooms and continue cooking, covered, 10 minutes, not under pressure. Add peas and cook 5 minutes. Serve, garnished with parsley, over rice.

Wet Clay Cooker Method
Combine all ingredients, except butter, onions, mushrooms and peas, in a pre-soaked unglazed clay cooker, reducing beef stock and Burgundy to 1/4 pint each. Cover and place in a cold oven. Turn oven to 400° and bake 1 hour and 15 minutes. Add butter, onions and mushrooms, cover and bake 15 minutes. Remove from oven, add peas, cover and let stand 10 minutes. Serve, garnished with parsley, over rice.

BEEF WITH ONIONS

Serves 2
2 onions, thinly sliced
2 tablespoons butter
6 to 8 tablespoons tomato sauce
6 to 8 tablespoons beef stock
6 to 8 tablespoons dry white wine
4 slices boiled beef (use any leftover boiled beef)
salt and freshly ground pepper to taste
2 tablespoons bread crumbs
accompaniments:
    French bread
    tossed green salad

In a frying pan, sauté onions in butter until golden brown, about 5 minutes. Add the tomato sauce, stock and wine and lay the beef slices on top. Simmer for 15 minutes. Salt and pepper lightly. Spoon sauce in the pan over meat with some of the onions. Sprinkle with bread crumbs and place in a preheated 375° oven for 10 minutes or until top is crusty. Serve with French bread and green salad.

BEEF

POT ROAST, VIENNESE STYLE

Serves 6 to 8
1 3-1/2 to 4-pound beef pot roast
2 tablespoons butter
1 teaspoon salt
1/2 teaspoon freshly ground pepper
1 onion, chopped
2 carrots, chopped
2 turnips, chopped
4 dried figs, chopped
1/2 pint white wine
1/2 pint beef stock
8 new potatoes
4 gingersnaps, crushed

Top-of-the-Stove Method
(flameproof casserole or heavy saucepan may be used)
Brown the meat on all sides in butter. Add salt, pepper, onion, carrots, turnips and figs. Pour in the wine and stock. Cover and simmer for 1-1/2 hours or until meat is tender. Add potatoes and simmer 20 minutes or until tender. Stir in the gingersnaps to thicken juices.

Slow Cooker Method
Brown meat on all sides in butter in a frying pan or slow cooker with a browning unit. Put carrots, turnips and potatoes in bottom of slow cooker and place roast on top. Add remaining ingredients, except gingersnaps, reducing wine and stock to a generous 1/4 pint each. Cover and cook on low 8 to 10 hours. Add gingersnaps and cook on high, uncovered, until thickened.

Pressure Cooker Method
In a pressure cooker brown meat on all sides in butter. Add salt, pepper, onion, wine, stock and 1/4 pint water. Cover and bring to full pressure. When steam appears, reduce heat and cook on low 25 minutes. Reduce pressure completely, add remaining vegetables and figs, cover and simmer 20 minutes or until tender, not under pressure. Add gingersnaps and cook, uncovered, until thickened.

Wet Clay Cooker Method
Combine all ingredients, reducing wine and stock to a generous 1/4 pint each, in a pre-soaked unglazed clay cooker. Cover and place in a cold oven. Turn oven to 400° and bake 1-1/2 hours or until meat is tender. Remove from oven and let stand 10 minutes.

POT ROAST, CREOLE STYLE

Serves 6 to 8
2 slices bacon, diced
1 teaspoon freshly ground pepper
1 3-1/2 to 4-pound beef pot roast
1 or more fresh green chili peppers, seeded and
   finely chopped, or
1/2 teaspoon crushed dried red chili peppers
1 bay leaf
1/2 teaspoon dried thyme
1 pound ripe tomatoes, peeled and diced
1/2 teaspoon sugar
1 celery rib, chopped
1 onion, chopped
2 cloves garlic, finely chopped
2 tablespoons chopped parsley or coriander
accompaniment: freshly cooked rice or French
   bread

Top-of-the-Stove Method
(flameproof casserole or heavy saucepan may be used)
Cook the bacon long enough to release the fat; do not brown. Remove bacon pieces with a slotted spoon and set aside. Pepper the meat and brown on all sides in drippings. Add the remaining ingredients. Cover and simmer for 2 hours or until tender. Fifteen minutes before the roast is done, add the bacon pieces to the pan. Slice the meat and serve with pan juices and rice or French bread.

Slow Cooker Method
Cook the bacon long enough to release the fat in a frying pan or slow cooker with a browning unit. Remove bacon with a slotted spoon; set aside. Pepper the meat and brown on all sides in drippings. Add the remaining ingredients, cover and cook on low 8 to 10 hours. Add reserved bacon pieces, cover, turn on high and cook 15 minutes. Slice the meat and serve with pan juices and rice or French bread.

Pressure Cooker Method
In a pressure cooker cook the bacon long enough to release the fat; remove bacon pieces with a slotted spoon and set aside. Pepper the meat and brown on all sides in drippings. Add the remaining ingredients with 1/2 pint water. Cover and bring to full pressure. When steam appears, reduce heat and cook on low 30 minutes. Reduce pressure completely and let stand covered 10 to 15 minutes to blend flavors. Stir in bacon pieces. Slice meat and serve with pan juices and rice or French bread.

Wet Clay Cooker Method
Pepper the meat and place in a pre-soaked unglazed clay cooker. Add remaining ingredients, cover and place in a cold oven. Turn oven to 400° and bake for 1-1/2 hours. Remove from oven and let stand 10 minutes. Slice the meat and serve with pan juices and rice or French bread.

BEEF

CALIFORNIA POT ROAST

Serves 8 to 10
1 4- to 5-pound beef pot roast
2 teaspoons salt
1/4 teaspoon freshly ground pepper
1/4 teaspoon ground ginger
2 tablespoons each butter and corn oil
2 cloves garlic, finely chopped
3 onions, chopped
1/2 pint dry red wine
1/2 pint beef stock
6 ounces pitted prunes, soaked in 1/2 pint water
1/2 pound courgettes, cut into chunks
4 ounces small button mushrooms
4 ounces pitted black olives
accompaniment: French bread

Top-of-the-Stove Method

Rub roast with salt, pepper and ginger. Brown on all sides in a flameproof casserole in butter and oil. Add garlic, onions, wine and stock. Cover and cook over low heat for 1 hour, turning meat occasionally. Add prunes and their liquid. Cover and continue cooking for 45 minutes or until roast is tender. Add courgettes, mushrooms and olives and simmer 15 minutes. Serve with French bread.

Slow Cooker Method

Rub the roast with the salt, pepper and ginger and brown on all sides in butter and oil in a frying pan or slow cooker with browning unit. Combine meat with remaining ingredients, except courgettes, mushrooms and olives, reducing stock by half and place in a slow cooker; cover and cook on low 8 to 10 hours. Add courgettes, mushrooms and olives, cover and cook on high 20 minutes. Serve with French bread.

Wet Clay Cooker Method

Combine all ingredients except courgettes, mushrooms and olives, reducing wine and stock by a quarter, in a pre-soaked unglazed clay cooker. Cover and place in a cold oven. Turn oven to 400° and bake 1-1/2 hours. Add courgettes, mushrooms and olives, cover and bake 15 minutes. Remove from oven and let stand 10 minutes. Serve with French bread.

BOILED BEEF AND SAUSAGE WITH VEGETABLES

Serves 6 to 8
1 5-pound beef brisket or silverside
1/2 pound lean salt pork, blanched
1 bay leaf
1/2 teaspoon dried thyme
8 peppercorns
2 onions, each stuck with 2 cloves
1 pound fresh pork or garlic sausages
6 carrots
4 celery ribs, halved
6 small turnips
2 swedes, quartered
1 head Savoy cabbage, cut in wedges
6 leeks
6 to 8 new potatoes
accompaniments: horseradish, Dijon-style mustard,
   dill pickles

Top-of-the-Stove Method
Place the beef and salt pork in a large soup pot with water to cover. Bring to a boil and skim any surface scum. Add bay leaf, thyme, peppercorns and onions. Lower heat, cover and simmer 1-1/2 hours. Add sausages and remaining vegetables and continue simmering for 30 minutes. Remove and slice the meats and place on a warm platter surrounded by the vegetables. Accompany with horseradish, mustard and dill pickles. Strain the broth and serve in cups.

Slow Cooker Method
Combine all ingredients with water to cover in a slow cooker and cook on low, covered, for 8 to 10 hours. Remove and slice the meats and place on a warm platter surrounded by the vegetables. Accompany with horseradish, mustard and pickles. Strain the broth and serve in cups.

BEEF

COTTAGE STEW

Serves 4

1-1/2 pounds lean stewing beef, cut into 1-inch
  cubes, dusted with
2 tablespoons flour
2 tablespoons each butter and corn oil
2 celery ribs with leaves, cut in chunks
1/2 pint beef stock
1/2 teaspoon salt
1/4 teaspoon freshly ground pepper
1/2 teaspoon each dried thyme and marjoram
1 teaspoon prepared mustard
2 tablespoons fresh lemon juice
3 tablespoons chopped parsley
accompaniment: toast, boiled noodles or potatoes

Top-of-the-Stove Method

Brown the meat in a saucepan in butter and oil.
Add celery, stock, salt, pepper, thyme, marjoram
and mustard. Cover and simmer for 1-1/2 hours or
until meat is tender. Stir in the lemon juice and
parsley and serve with toast, noodles or potatoes.

Slow Cooker Method

Brown meat in butter and oil in a frying pan or
slow cooker with a browning unit. Combine meat
and remaining ingredients, except lemon juice and
parsley, and place in a slow cooker. Cover and
cook on low 6 to 8 hours. Stir in lemon juice and
parsley and serve with toast, noodles or potatoes.

Pressure Cooker Method

In a pressure cooker brown the meat in butter and
oil. Add remaining ingredients, except lemon juice
and parsley, adding 1/2 pint water. Cover and
bring to full pressure. When steam appears, reduce
heat and cook on low 20 minutes. Reduce pressure
completely and let stand 10 to 15 minutes to blend
flavors. Stir in lemon juice and parsley and serve
with toast, noodles or potatoes.

BEEF AND VEGETABLES
WITH SOUR CREAM

Serves 4 to 6

1 pound lean minced beef
1 onion, chopped
2 tablespoons butter
2 potatoes, peeled and cut into 1/2-inch cubes
1 turnip, cut into 1/4-inch cubes
3 carrots, cut into 1/4-inch cubes
2 celery ribs, cut into 1/2-inch slices
1/4 teaspoon caraway seeds
1/4 teaspoon paprika
1 teaspoon salt

1/4 teaspoon freshly ground pepper
1/2 pint sour cream
1 tablespoon flour
garnish: 2 tablespoons chopped parsley

In a large frying pan sauté beef and onion in butter until browned, about 5 minutes. Add potatoes, turnip, carrots, celery, caraway seeds, paprika, salt and pepper. Cover and cook over medium heat for 15 minutes or until vegetables are tender. Combine sour cream and flour and add to the pan, stirring constantly. Heat through; do not boil. Serve from the pan immediately, garnished with parsley.

BEEF

BEEF-AND-KIDNEY STEW

Serves 6
1/4 pound mushrooms, halved
4 tablespoons butter
1 large onion, chopped
2 pounds lean stewing beef, cut into
    1-inch cubes, dusted with
4 tablespoons flour
4 lamb kidneys, thinly sliced
3/4 pint beef stock
2 tablespoons chopped parsley
1 teaspoon dried thyme
1/2 bay leaf
1/4 teaspoon freshly ground pepper
pinch of cayenne pepper
1 teaspoon Worcestershire sauce
4 potatoes, peeled and quartered
garnish: chopped parsley

Top-of-the-Stove Method
In a heavy pan, sauté mushrooms in 2 tablespoons of the butter for 5 minutes; remove and set aside. Add remaining butter and brown onions, beef and kidneys. Add remaining ingredients, except potatoes, and bring to a rapid boil. Reduce heat, cover and simmer 1 hour. Add potatoes, cover and simmer 20 minutes. Add reserved mushrooms, cover and cook 10 minutes. Garnish with parsley.

Slow Cooker Method
Sauté mushrooms in 2 tablespoons of the butter in a frying pan or slow cooker with browning unit for 5 minutes; remove and set aside. Add remaining butter and brown onions, beef and kidneys. Put potatoes in the bottom of a slow cooker and add meat mixture with remaining ingredients, reducing stock by a quarter. Cover and cook on low 6 to 8 hours. Add reserved mushrooms, cover and cook on high 15 minutes. Garnish with parsley.

Pressure Cooker Method

In a pressure cooker sauté the mushrooms in 2 tablespoons of the butter for 5 minutes. Remove and set aside. Add remaining butter and brown onions, beef and kidneys. Add remaining ingredients, except potatoes, with 1/2 pint water. Cover; bring to full pressure. When steam appears, reduce heat and cook on low 15 minutes. Reduce pressure completely, add potatoes, cover and simmer 20 minutes, not under pressure. Add reserved mushrooms; simmer 10 minutes. Garnish with parsley.

Wet Clay Cooker Method

Combine all ingredients, reducing stock by a quarter, in a pre-soaked unglazed clay cooker. Cover and place in a cold oven. Turn oven to 400° and bake 1-1/2 hours. Remove from oven and let stand 10 minutes. Garnish with parsley.

INDIAN CORN STEW

Serves 4

1 pound lean minced beef
1 onion, chopped
1 clove garlic, finely chopped
2 tablespoons lard
1 or more fresh green chili peppers,
  seeded and chopped, or
1/2 teaspoon crushed dried red chili peppers
1 sweet green pepper, chopped
3/4 pound fresh or frozen corn kernels
3 large ripe tomatoes, peeled and coarsely chopped
1 tablespoon sugar
1 teaspoon salt
1/2 teaspoon freshly ground pepper
accompaniment: French bread

In a frying pan, sauté meat, onion and garlic in lard until meat loses its redness. Add the chilies, sweet pepper, corn, tomatoes and seasonings. Cover and simmer for 20 minutes. Serve with crusty French bread.

BEEF

CORNED (SALTED) BEEF AND CABBAGE

Serves 4 to 6

1 4-pound salted beef brisket, soaked in cold
    water to cover for 2 hours to remove
    excess brine if necessary
1 bay leaf
6 peppercorns
1 onion, stuck with 2 cloves
1 carrot, sliced
1 celery rib, sliced
2 sprigs parsley
1/2 pint cider
6 carrots, halved crosswise
6 new potatoes
1 small head cabbage, cut into 4 to 6 wedges
accompaniments: Dijon-style mustard, horseradish,
    gherkin pickles

Top-of-the-Stove Method

Combine all ingredients in a soup pot except the halved carrots, potatoes and cabbage. Add enough water to cover. Bring to a rapid boil and skim off any surface scum. Lower heat, cover and simmer 1-1/2 hours or until tender. Remove corned beef to a platter and keep warm. Add halved carrots and the potatoes to pot and cook 15 minutes. Add cabbage and cook 15 minutes. Surround corned beef with vegetables. Serve with accompaniments.

Slow Cooker Method

Combine all ingredients, except cabbage, with water to cover and cook on low, covered, for 8 to 10 hours. Remove corned beef and vegetables to a platter and keep warm. Add cabbage to pot, cover and cook on high for 20 minutes. Place cabbage on platter with meat and vegetables. Serve with accompaniments.

Pressure Cooker Method

Place all ingredients except cabbage, halved carrots and potatoes in a pressure cooker with water to two-thirds capacity. Cover and bring to full pressure. When steam appears, reduce heat and cook on low 25 minutes. Reduce pressure completely, uncover and remove corned beef to a platter and keep warm. Add carrots and potatoes to pot, cover and cook 15 minutes, not under pressure. Add cabbage, cover and cook 15 minutes. Surround corned beef with vegetables. Serve with accompaniments.

MEATLOAF WITH POTATOES AND CHEESE FILLING

Serves 6
1 pound lean minced beef
1/2 pound minced veal
1 slice bread, trimmed and crumbled
6 to 8 tablespoons grated Parmesan cheese
4 tablespoons chopped parsley
1 onion, chopped
2 eggs
6 to 8 tablespoons milk
1 teaspoon salt
1/2 teaspoon freshly ground pepper
3 tablespoons olive oil
3/4 pound mashed cooked potatoes
1/2 pound mozzarella or mild Cheddar cheese, sliced

Combine all ingredients except the oil, potatoes and sliced cheese and mix well. Place half of this mixture in a large loaf tin or baking dish which has been brushed with 1 tablespoon of the olive oil. Layer the potatoes and then the cheese on top of the meat mixture. Top with remaining meat mixture, covering potatoes and cheese completely. Brush top with the remaining oil and bake in a preheated 350° oven for 1 hour or until meat is brown on top, but not dry.

SWEET AND SOUR BEEF WITH FRUIT

Serves 4 to 6
3 onions, sliced
4 tablespoons butter
2 large tomatoes, peeled, seeded and diced
1-1/2 pounds round steak, cut into 1/2-inch dice, or
1-1/2 pounds lean minced beef
1 teaspoon salt
1/2 teaspoon freshly ground pepper
1/2 pint beef stock
2 pears, peeled and sliced
2 peaches, peeled and sliced, or
6 apricots, peeled and sliced
6 plums, peeled and sliced
3 potatoes, peeled and diced
3 tablespoons raisins
garnish: toasted slivered almonds

In a saucepan brown onions in butter; add tomatoes and cook for 2 minutes. Add beef and cook and stir for 2 minutes. Add salt, pepper and stock. Simmer, covered, for 30 minutes. Add fruit and potatoes and cook for 15 to 20 minutes or until potatoes are tender. Add raisins and serve garnished with almonds.

BEEF

CHILE CON CARNE

Serves 6 to 8

2 pounds stewing beef, cut into 1/2-inch cubes, or
1 pound each stewing beef and lean pork,
    cut into 1/2-inch cubes
1 onion, chopped
3 cloves garlic, finely chopped
2 tablespoons lard
1-1/2 pounds ripe tomatoes, peeled and chopped
4 tablespoons compound chili powder, mixed with
1 tablespoon flour
1 tablespoon finely chopped fresh oregano, or
1 teaspoon dried oregano
1/2 teaspoon ground cumin
2 bay leaves
1 teaspoon salt
4 ounces pitted black olives
garnishes: chopped onions, finely chopped fresh
    green chilies, chopped coriander
accompaniment: warm tortillas (following)

Top-of-the-Stove Method
(flameproof casserole or heavy saucepan may be used)

Brown meat, onion and garlic in lard. Add tomatoes, chili powder-flour mixture, oregano, cumin, bay leaves and salt. Bring just to a boil, lower heat, cover and simmer for 2 hours. Add olives and simmer another 10 minutes. Garnish and serve with tortillas.

Slow Cooker Method

Brown the meat, onion and garlic in lard in a frying pan or slow cooker with browning unit. Combine meat mixture and remaining ingredients except olives in a slow cooker. Cover and cook on low 6 to 8 hours. Add olives, cover and cook on high 10 minutes. Garnish and serve with tortillas.

Pressure Cooker Method

In a pressure cooker brown meat, onion and garlic in lard. Add the tomatoes, chili powder-flour mixture, oregano, cumin, bay leaves, salt and 1/2 pint water. Cover and bring to full pressure. When steam appears, reduce heat and cook on low for 25 minutes. Reduce pressure completely, uncover, add olives and cook 10 minutes, not under pressure. Garnish and serve with tortillas.

BEEF

Wet Clay Cooker Method
Combine all ingredients except olives in a pre-soaked unglazed clay cooker. Cover and place in a cold oven. Turn oven to 400° and bake 1-1/2 hours. Remove from oven, add olives, cover and let stand 10 minutes. Garnish and serve with tortillas.

Note To prepare chile with beans, add a 1-pound can of red kidney beans, drained, to the pot after prescribed cooking time and just heat through before serving.

TORTILLAS

Mix together 6 ounces each flour and cornmeal, 4 tablespoons corn oil and 3/4 teaspoon salt. Gradually add enough lukewarm water (about 1/4 pint) to make a firm, pliable dough. Turn out on to a floured board and knead vigorously for at least 3 minutes. Divide dough into 12 pieces and roll each piece into a ball. Let stand 15 minutes. On a floured board roll each ball into a pancake about 6 inches in diameter. Fry on a lightly greased griddle or heavy frying pan, turning 2 or 3 times, until cooked but not browned. Stack and leave to cool.
Makes 12 tortillas.

BOILED BEEF SALAD

Serves 4
1/2 pound diced boiled beef
1 small onion, diced
2 celery ribs, diced
1 large red or green pepper (or half and half), diced
1 large potato, peeled, boiled and diced
6 to 8 tablespoons chopped parsley
1 tablespoon Dijon-style mustard
1 teaspoon salt
1/2 teaspoon freshly ground pepper
5 tablespoons olive oil
3 to 4 tablespoons wine vinegar
lettuce leaves
2 large tomatoes, cut into wedges
2 hard-boiled eggs, cut into quarters

Combine all ingredients, except for lettuce, tomatoes and eggs, and toss well. Place lettuce leaves on individual cold salad plates, spoon beef mixture on top and surround with tomatoes and eggs.

BEEF

RED FLANNEL HASH

Serves 4

1 medium-sized onion, chopped
6 tablespoons butter
3 medium-sized beetroots, cooked and diced
1 large potato, peeled, boiled and diced
1/4 pound fresh or salted boiled beef, diced
salt and freshly ground pepper to taste
2 tablespoons double cream

In a frying pan sauté onion in half the butter until transparent. Add beetroots, potato and diced beef, stirring well to combine with the onion. Season with salt and pepper and cook over low heat for 10 minutes. Drizzle cream over the hash and dot with the remaining butter. Put under a pre-heated grill for 5 minutes or until top is crusty and brown.

STUFFED CABBAGE, UKRAINIAN STYLE

Serves 4 to 6

1-1/2 pounds lean minced beef
2 ounces long-grain rice, cooked
1 teaspoon salt
1/2 teaspoon freshly ground pepper
8 to 10 large cabbage leaves, blanched
    until wilted
1/2 pint tomato juice
1 6-ounce can tomato paste
1 onion, chopped
4 tablespoons vinegar
1/2 pint water
2 tablespoons sugar
8 gingersnaps, crushed

Oven Method

Combine the meat, rice, salt and pepper. Fill each cabbage leaf with about 6 to 8 tablespoons meat-rice mixture, fold in sides like an envelope, roll up and place seam side down in a shallow baking dish or casserole. Combine remaining ingredients and pour over cabbage rolls. Cover and bake in a preheated 325° oven for 1 hour.

Slow Cooker Method

Prepare stuffed cabbage rolls as directed for oven method. Place seam side down in a slow cooker. Combine remaining ingredients, reducing water by a quarter, and pour over cabbage rolls. Cover and cook on low 6 to 8 hours.

BEEF

TRANSYLVANIA VEAL STEW

Serves 6 to 8
2 pounds boneless veal, cut into 1-inch cubes,
  dusted with
2 tablespoons flour
3 tablespoons each butter and corn oil
2 onions, finely chopped
3 potatoes, peeled and thinly sliced
2 courgettes, sliced
2 green peppers, sliced
3 tablespoons chopped parsley
1/4 pound green beans, cut up
salt and freshly ground pepper to taste
1 pound ripe tomatoes, sliced
1/2 pint sour cream

Oven Method
Sauté veal in butter and oil in a large flameproof casserole until lightly browned. Add the onions and cook until browned. Remove from heat. Add potatoes, courgettes, peppers, parsley, green beans, salt and pepper. Top with sliced tomatoes. Cover and bake in a preheated 350° oven for 1 hour or until tender. Remove from oven and stir in sour cream.

Slow Cooker Method
Sauté veal in butter and oil in a frying pan or a slow cooker with browning unit. Add onions and cook until browned. Put the potatoes in the bottom of a slow cooker. Add the browned meat, onions and remaining ingredients, except the sour cream, placing the tomatoes on top. Cover and cook on low 6 to 8 hours. Stir in sour cream when ready to serve.

STUFFED BREAST OF VEAL

Serves 6
1 3- to 4-pound breast of veal
1 small onion, chopped
3 tablespoons butter
1 crusty French bread roll, soaked in water,
   squeezed to remove excess water and crumbled
2 ounces ham, diced
5 ounces cooked peas or asparagus tips
2 tablespoons chopped parsley
2 eggs, beaten
1 teaspoon salt
1/2 teaspoon freshly ground pepper
1 teaspoon paprika
1/2 pint tomato juice
1/4 pint sour cream

Make a pocket in the breast of veal. Sauté the onion in butter until transparent. Add the bread crumbs, ham, peas and parsley and blend well for 2 minutes. Remove from heat and mix the eggs into the bread mixture. Sprinkle the breast with salt, pepper and paprika inside and out. Stuff with bread mixture and sew up or skewer opening. Put in a roasting tin and roast in a preheated 325° oven for 1-1/2 hours or until meat is tender and brown. Baste occasionally with tomato juice. When veal is cooked, remove it from pan and add sour cream to pan juices, blending well. Slice veal and spoon sauce over slices.

LIVER DUMPLINGS

Serves 6
1-1/2 pounds calf's or ox liver
1 large onion
3 tablespoons chopped chives
3 tablespoons chopped parsley
5 slices white bread, crusts removed
2 eggs
2 tablespoons flour
2 teaspoons salt
1/2 teaspoon freshly ground pepper
1/4 teaspoon freshly grated nutmeg
accompaniments:
   crisply cooked bacon
   sliced tomatoes or coleslaw

Mince liver with onion, chives, parsley and bread. Add eggs, flour, salt, pepper and nutmeg and mix well. Bring 4 pints water to a boil in a large saucepan. Drop liver mixture by spoonfuls into boiling water, rinsing spoon in hot water each time. Cover pan and simmer for 10 minutes. Remove dumplings with slotted spoon and place on heated platter. Serve with accompaniments.

BEEF

BRAISED OXTAILS, SPANISH STYLE

Serves 6
3 to 4 pounds oxtails, disjointed
3 tablespoons olive oil
2 onions, chopped
2 cloves garlic, finely chopped
1 tablespoon flour
3/4 pint beef stock
1/2 pint dry red wine
6 to 8 tablespoons puréed fresh or canned toma-
    toes, or tomato juice
6 black peppercorns
1/2 teaspoon dried oregano
1 dried red chili pepper, seeded and chopped
2 whole cloves
2 carrots, chopped
1 sweet red pepper, chopped
1 tablespoon chopped parsley
2 potatoes, peeled and cut into chunks
salt and freshly ground pepper to taste

Top-of-the-Stove Method
In a heavy pan, brown oxtails on all sides in oil.
Add onions and garlic and cook 5 minutes. Sprinkle flour over the meat, blend well, and cook 2
minutes. Add stock, wine, tomato purée, peppercorns, oregano, chili pepper and cloves. Cover and
simmer 1-1/2 hours or until meat is almost tender.
Add remaining ingredients and cook 20 minutes.

Slow Cooker Method
Brown oxtails on all sides in oil in a frying pan or
slow cooker with a browning unit. Add onions and
garlic and cook 5 minutes. Sprinkle flour over the
meat, blend well and cook 2 minutes. Reduce
stock and wine by a quarter and add with all the
remaining ingredients and the meat to a slow cooker,
placing potatoes in the bottom. Cover and cook on
low 8 to 10 hours.

Pressure Cooker Method
In a pressure cooker brown oxtails on all sides in oil. Add onions and garlic and cook 5 minutes. Sprinkle flour over the meat, blend well, and cook 2 minutes. Add stock, wine, tomato purée, pepper-corns, oregano, chili pepper, cloves and 1/2 pint water. Cover and bring to full pressure. When steam appears, reduce heat and cook on low 30 minutes. Reduce pressure completely, uncover, add remaining ingredients and cook 20 minutes, not under pressure.

Wet Clay Cooker Method
Sprinkle oxtails with flour. Place in a pre-soaked unglazed clay cooker and add onions, garlic, only three-quarters of the beef stock and wine, the tomato purée, peppercorns, oregano, chili pepper and cloves. Cover and place in a cold oven. Turn oven to 400° and bake 1-1/2 hours. Add remaining ingredients, cover and bake 20 minutes. Remove from oven and let stand 10 minutes.

BEEF

CARIBBEAN OXTAIL STEW

Serves 6
3 pounds oxtails, disjointed
2 tablespoons corn oil
1 tablespoon compound chili powder
1 tablespoon dry mustard
1 tablespoon cornflour
1 teaspoon salt
2 tablespoons fresh lemon juice
3/4 pint fresh orange juice
6 to 8 tablespoons raisins
1 green pepper, cut into strips
4 ounces pitted black olives
3 celery ribs, thinly sliced
1 teaspoon freshly grated orange peel
garnish: watercress sprigs
accompaniment: freshly cooked rice

Top-of-the-Stove Method
In a heavy pan, brown the oxtails in the oil. Mix together the chili powder, mustard, cornflour, salt and lemon and orange juices. Add mixture to the meat and bring just to a boil. Lower heat, cover and simmer 2 hours. Add the raisins, pepper, olives and celery. Cover and cook 15 minutes. Stir in grated orange peel, garnish with watercress and serve over rice.

Slow Cooker Method
Brown the oxtails in oil in a frying pan or a slow cooker with a browning unit. Mix together chili powder, mustard, cornflour, salt and lemon and orange juices, reducing the orange juice by a quarter. Add to slow cooker with the oxtails, cover and cook on low 8 to 10 hours. Add the raisins, pepper, olives and celery, cover, turn on high and cook 20 minutes. Stir in grated orange peel, garnish with watercress and serve over rice.

Pressure Cooker Method
In a pressure cooker brown the oxtails in the oil. Mix together the chili powder, mustard, cornflour, salt and lemon and orange juices with 1/2 pint water. Add mixture to pressure cooker, cover and bring to full pressure. When steam appears, reduce heat and cook on low 30 minutes. Reduce pressure completely, uncover and add the raisins, pepper, olives and celery. Cover and cook 15 minutes, not under pressure. Stir in grated orange peel, garnish with watercress and serve over rice.

Wet Clay Cooker Method
Place oxtails in a pre-soaked unglazed clay cooker. Combine oil, chili powder, mustard, cornflour, salt and lemon and orange juices, reducing orange juice by a quarter, and add to clay cooker. Cover and place in a cold oven. Turn oven to 400° and bake 1-1/2 hours. Add the raisins, pepper, olives and celery, cover and bake 10 minutes. Remove from oven; let stand 10 minutes. Stir in orange peel, garnish and serve over rice.

BOILED TONGUE DINNER

Serves 6

1 ox tongue, about 3 pounds
1 pound marrow bones, cut into 1-1/2-inch pieces
1 clove garlic
1 onion, stuck with 2 cloves
1/2 teaspoon dried rosemary
1 bay leaf
1 teaspoon salt
1/2 teaspoon freshly ground pepper
6 turnips, cut into chunks
3 celery ribs, with some leaves
12 small boiling onions
6 new potatoes
6 whole leeks, white parts only
accompaniments: horseradish, Dijon-style mustard

Top-of-the-Stove Method
Combine tongue, marrow bones, garlic, onion, rosemary, bay leaf, salt, pepper and 5 pints water in a large soup pot. Simmer for 1-1/2 hours. Add vegetables and cook 20 minutes or until vegetables are tender. Remove tongue from pot, let stand 10 minutes, skin and slice. Place on a warmed platter.

Remove vegetables and marrow bones from broth with a slotted spoon and place on platter with tongue. Serve with accompaniments. Broth may be strained and served separately.

Slow Cooker Method
Combine all ingredients with water to cover in a slow cooker, placing potatoes and turnips in the bottom. Cover and cook on low 8 to 10 hours. Remove tongue from pot and proceed as directed for top-of-the-stove method.

Pressure Cooker Method
Place the tongue, marrow bones, garlic, onion, rosemary, bay leaf, salt and pepper in a pressure cooker with water to two-thirds capacity. Cover and bring to full pressure. When steam appears, reduce heat and cook on low 20 minutes. Reduce pressure completely, uncover, add all remaining ingredients, cover and cook 30 minutes or until vegetables are tender, not under pressure. Let stand 10 minutes to blend flavors. Remove tongue from pot and proceed as directed for top-of-the-stove method.

BEEF

TONGUE STUFFED WITH HAM AND SAUSAGE

Serves 6 to 8

1 3- to 4-pound ox tongue
6 to 8 tablespoons fresh lemon juice
1/2 pound minced veal
1/2 pound pork sausage meat
6 to 8 tablespoons finely chopped ham
2 eggs, beaten
1-1/2 teaspoons salt
1/2 teaspoon freshly ground pepper
2 tablespoons chopped coriander or parsley
6 to 8 tablespoons bread crumbs
1 teaspoon dried oregano
1 bay leaf
1 onion, quartered
6 peppercorns
1 teaspoon salt
1/2 pint dry white wine
1 pound ripe tomatoes, peeled and diced
3 ounces rice
accompaniment: Fresh Tomato Sauce, following

Top-of-the-Stove Method

Wash tongue and dry with paper towels. Make a deep slit the length of the underside almost to the tip. Make several lengthwise slashes in the flesh. Rub lemon juice into tongue and let stand 10 minutes. Make a forcemeat by combining the veal, sausage, ham, eggs, salt, pepper, coriander and bread crumbs. Pile onto tongue and truss sides of tongue together with heavy thread. Place stuffed tongue in a large soup pot with oregano, bay leaf, onion, peppercorns, salt, wine and water to cover (about 3 pints). Cover and simmer for 2 hours. Remove tongue, reserving liquid. Let tongue stand 10 minutes, then skin and slice. Strain the reserved liquid and add tomatoes and rice. Simmer 20 minutes and serve as soup, either with tongue or as another course. Serve tongue with Fresh Tomato Sauce. (This dish is also delicious served cold.)

Slow Cooker Method

Prepare stuffed tongue as directed for top-of-the-stove method. Place the tongue with all ingredients except tomatoes and rice in a slow cooker, adding water to cover. Cover and cook on low 8 to 10 hours. Remove tongue and let stand 10 minutes; then skin and slice. Strain the cooking liquid and return to slow cooker. Add tomatoes and rice, cover and cook on high 20 minutes. Serve as directed for top-of-the-stove method.

FRESH TOMATO SAUCE

Makes 3/4 pint

1 pound ripe tomatoes, peeled and chopped
2 or more fresh green chili peppers,
    seeded and chopped, or
1/2 teaspoon or more crushed dried red chili
    peppers
2 tablespoons olive oil
2 tablespoons red wine vinegar

1 small onion, finely chopped
1 clove garlic, finely chopped
1/2 teaspoon dried oregano
1 tablespoon chopped coriander
salt and freshly ground pepper to taste

Combine all ingredients and refrigerate for 2 to 3 hours to allow flavors to blend.

TRIPES A LA NORMANDE
(Tripe with Calf's Feet)

Serves 4 to 6

4 pounds honeycomb tripe, cut into 2-inch
    squares and blanched
2 calf's feet, blanched
3/4 pint dry white wine
1-1/2 pints beef stock, heated
2 onions, each stuck with 2 cloves
4 leeks, white parts only
2 cloves garlic
2 celery ribs, halved with some leaves
1 bay leaf
1/2 teaspoon dried thyme
4 tablespoons chopped parsley
2 carrots, halved

1/2 pound button mushrooms
2 teaspoons salt
1 teaspoon freshly ground pepper
accompaniments:
    Dijon-style mustard
    boiled new potatoes or French bread

Combine all the ingredients in an earthenware or other large heatproof casserole. Cover with a tight-fitting lid and place in a preheated 325° oven for 4 hours or until meat is tender. Remove meat from calf's feet and return meat to the casserole. Continue cooking, uncovered, for 1 hour or until liquid has reduced to a saucelike consistency. Serve very hot with Dijon-style mustard and boiled new potatoes or French bread.

MEAL IN A DISH PASTRIES

PASTRY FOR TWO-CRUST PIE

Makes 2 8- or 9-inch crusts
8 ounces unbleached white flour
1 teaspoon salt
6 ounces white vegetable fat or lard, or half butter
    and half vegetable fat
5 to 6 tablespoons cold water

Put flour and salt in a bowl and cut in vegetable fat with a pastry blender or two knives until mixture is crumbly. Sprinkle water over mixture, mixing lightly with a fork. Form into a ball with hands and divide in half. Roll out each half on lightly floured board to a thickness of 1/8 inch. Fit into pie dishes or on top of pie according to recipe. For one crust, halve the above ingredients and proceed as directed.

SCONE DOUGH

Makes 1 10-inch crust
6 ounces unbleached white flour
2 teaspoons baking powder
1/2 teaspoon salt
1-1/2 ounces butter
3 tablespoons corn oil
1 egg, beaten
cold water

Sift the flour, baking powder and salt together. Cut in butter with a pastry blender or 2 knives until mixture is crumbly. Add oil, egg and just enough cold water to form dough into a ball with hands. Roll out 1/4 inch thick. May be used for top crust of pot pies or deep-dish pies.

113

MEAL IN A DISH PASTRIES

CRAB QUICHE

Serves 4 to 6
half recipe Pastry for Two-Crust Pie, page 113
1/2 pound cooked flaked crab meat
1/4 pound Emmenthal cheese, grated
3 eggs
8 fluid ounces double cream
3 tablespoons chopped chives
1/2 teaspoon salt
1/8 teaspoon white pepper
chopped fresh dill

Prepare 1 9-inch pie shell and prick all over with fork tines. Bake for 5 minutes in a preheated 350° oven. Remove crust from oven and turn oven to 375°. Sprinkle crab meat over crust and top with cheese. Mix together remaining ingredients except dill and pour mixture over crab and cheese. Sprinkle dill on top and bake at 375° for 45 minutes.

QUICHE LORRAINE

Serves 4 to 6
half recipe Pastry for Two-Crust Pie, page 113
6 thick slices bacon, cooked crisp, drained
   and crumbled
3 eggs
1 tablespoon flour
pinch of freshly grated nutmeg
1/4 teaspoon salt
1/8 teaspoon freshly ground pepper
1/4 pint milk
6 tablespoons single cream
2 tablespoons butter, melted

Prepare 1 9-inch pastry shell and prick all over with fork tines. Bake for 5 minutes in a preheated 350° oven. Remove crust from oven and turn oven to 375°. Distribute bacon pieces in pie shell. Beat together remaining ingredients and pour over bacon. Bake in a preheated 375° oven for 30 to 35 minutes or until custard is set and top is lightly browned. Serve warm.

VEAL PASTIES

Makes 8 pasties; serves 4
Pastry for Two-Crust Pie, page 113
1 pound minced veal
2 hard-boiled eggs, chopped
4 tablespoons chopped pitted prunes
4 tablespoons chopped pitted dates
3 tablespoons currants
3 tablespoons pine nuts or
    slivered blanched almonds
1/2 teaspoon fennel seeds
1/4 teaspoon each ground cinnamon and ginger
1/8 teaspoon freshly grated nutmeg

Prepare pastry dough and set aside. Combine all remaining ingredients for the filling and set aside. Divide the pastry dough into 8 equal portions and roll out each portion on a lightly floured board into a 6-inch round. Divide filling into 8 portions and place a portion on each pastry round. Fold over dough and crimp edges. Place pasties on a baking sheet and bake in a preheated 375° oven for 25 minutes or until golden.

CORNISH PASTIES

Makes 8 pasties; serves 4
Pastry for Two-Crust Pie, page 113
1-1/2 pounds lean minced beef
1 potato, peeled and finely diced
1 onion, finely diced
6 to 8 tablespoons chopped parsley
1 teaspoon salt
1/4 teaspoon freshly ground pepper

Prepare pastry dough and set aside. Combine all remaining ingredients for the filling and set aside. Divide the pastry dough into 8 equal portions and roll out each portion on a lightly floured board into a 6-inch round. Divide filling into 8 portions and place a portion on each pastry round. Fold over dough and crimp edges. Place pasties on a baking sheet and bake in a preheated 375° oven for 25 minutes or until golden.

MEAL IN A DISH PASTRIES

SWISS CHEESE PIE

Serves 4 to 6
half recipe Pastry for Two-Crust Pie, page 113
1/2 pound Emmenthal cheese, grated
1 tablespoon flour
3 eggs, beaten
1/4 pint milk
6 tablespoons single cream
pinch of freshly grated nutmeg

Prepare 1 9-inch pastry shell and prick all over with fork tines. Bake for 5 minutes in a preheated 350° oven. Remove crust from oven and turn oven to 375°. Mix the cheese with the flour and spread evenly over the pie shell. Combine the eggs and cream and pour over cheese mixture. Grate some nutmeg on top and bake in a preheated 375° oven for 30 to 35 minutes or until center is set. Serve warm.

CHICKEN PIE

Serves 4 to 6
Pastry for Two-Crust Pie, page 113
melted butter
1 pound cooked chicken, diced
salt and freshly ground pepper
1/4 teaspoon freshly grated nutmeg
3 eggs, beaten
6 to 8 tablespoons dry white wine
scant 1/2 pint cold rich chicken stock
4 hard-boiled eggs, chopped
6 ounces coarsely chopped cooked artichoke
    hearts or asparagus tips
2 tablespoons chopped spring onions

Prepare pastry dough and line a deep 9-inch pie dish with half the pastry. Brush with melted butter. Combine remaining ingredients, blending well, and pour into the pie shell. Roll out remaining dough and place on top, crimping edges. Make several slits in top of pastry and bake in a preheated 425° oven for 10 minutes. Lower heat to 325° and continue baking for 30 minutes or until golden. Serve hot or cold.

PORK AND APPLE PIE

Serves 4 or 5
Pastry for Two-Crust Pie, page 113
4 tart apples, peeled and sliced
1 pound lean minced pork
1/2 teaspoon dried thyme
1 tablespoon brown sugar
1/4 teaspoon powdered sage
1 teaspoon salt
1/4 teaspoon freshly ground pepper
2 tablespoons butter
1 egg, beaten with
1 teaspoon milk
accompaniments: freshly grated horseradish,
    sour cream

Prepare pastry dough and line a deep 9-inch pie dish with half the pastry. Combine the apples, pork, thyme, sugar, sage, salt and pepper and place mixture in pie shell; dot with butter. Roll out remaining dough and place on top, crimping edges. Make several slits in top of pastry. Brush with egg-milk mixture and bake in a preheated 400° oven for 1 hour. Serve at room temperature with accompaniments.

POTATO PIE

Makes 2 pies; serves 8 or more
Pastry for Two-Crust Pie, page 113
1 pound cottage cheese
1 pound potatoes, peeled, cooked and mashed
6 to 8 tablespoons sour cream
3 eggs
1 teaspoon salt
1/8 teaspoon cayenne pepper
6 to 8 tablespoons chopped spring onions
6 to 8 tablespoons grated Parmesan cheese

Prepare 2 9-inch pastry shells and set aside. Put cottage cheese through a sieve or whirl in a blender until smooth. Blend potatoes into cottage cheese and beat in sour cream, eggs, salt and cayenne. Stir in onions and Parmesan cheese. Spoon half of mixture into each pastry shell. Bake in a preheated 425° oven for 45 minutes or until golden.

Variation

For a Bacon-and-Potato Pie, add 6 slices bacon, crisply cooked and crumbled, to cottage cheese-potato mixture.

MEAL IN A DISH PASTRIES

AUBERGINE-AND-MACARONI PIE

Serves 6
Scone Dough, page 113
1 small aubergine, peeled and cubed
2 tablespoons vinegar
1 onion, chopped
3 tablespoons olive oil
6 to 8 tablespoons tomato paste
1/2 pound minced beef
2 chicken livers, parboiled 1 minute and finely
    chopped
4 ounces curd or cottage cheese
1 teaspoon dried oregano
1/2 pound macaroni, cooked al dente
2 ounces mild Cheddar, grated
1 hard-boiled egg, sliced
1 egg, beaten

Prepare scone dough and set aside. Soak aubergine
in water to cover and vinegar for 15 minutes; drain
and pat dry. Sauté aubergine with onion in oil. Mix
1/4 pint water with tomato paste and add to aubergine mixture. Mix minced beef and chicken livers;
add to aubergine mixture and simmer 5 minutes;
Remove from heat, add curd cheese and oregano
and mix well. Layer half of macaroni, aubergine
sauce and grated cheese in a buttered 3-pint casserole. Top with egg slices and repeat layers, ending
with grated cheese. Pour beaten egg over all. Roll
out pastry 1/4 inch thick and top casserole. Make
several slits in top of pastry and bake in a preheated 375° oven for 45 minutes or until top is
golden.

ROAST BEEF PIE

Serves 4
Scone Dough, page 113
1 small onion, chopped
1 clove garlic, finely chopped
4 ounces mushrooms, thinly sliced
4 tablespoons finely chopped green pepper
3 tablespoons roast beef drippings or butter
3 tablespoons flour
1 teaspoon salt
1/2 teaspoon freshly ground pepper
pinch each of dried thyme, ground cloves and
    freshly grated nutmeg
3/4 pint beef stock
1 pound fresh peas, shelled
1 large carrot, sliced
1 medium-size potato, peeled and cubed
2 tablespoons chopped sweet pickle
1 tablespoon capers
1/2 pound cooked roast beef, cubed

Prepare scone dough and set aside. In a 2-pint
flameproof casserole sauté the onion, garlic, mushrooms and pepper in the drippings for 3 minutes.
Sprinkle with flour and seasonings and cook over
low heat until well blended. Add the stock and
vegetables and cook 10 minutes or until vegetables
are just tender. Remove from heat and add remaining ingredients. Roll out dough 1/4 inch thick and
top casserole. Make several slits in top of pastry
and bake pie in a preheated 425° oven for 30
minutes or until crust is golden.

KIDNEY-SAUSAGE-AND-VEGETABLE PIE

Serves 4
Scone Dough, page 113
1 pound lamb or veal kidneys, suet removed
   and reserved
2 tablespoons flour
2 tablespoons butter
1/2 pound pork sausage meat
1/4 teaspoon powdered sage
1/2 teaspoon dried marjoram
1 small onion, chopped
1 celery rib with leaves, chopped
1 potato, peeled and diced
1 large carrot, thinly sliced
1 pound fresh peas, shelled
1/4 pint water
4 tablespoons dry sherry
1/2 teaspoon salt
1/4 teaspoon freshly ground pepper
1/8 teaspoon cayenne pepper

Prepare dough and set aside. Finely chop enough of reserved suet to make 1 tablespoon. Slice kidneys and dust with the flour. Sauté kidneys in suet and butter in a 3-pint flameproof casserole. Add remaining ingredients, bring to a gentle boil, cover and simmer 20 minutes. Remove from heat. Roll out scone dough 1/2 inch thick and top casserole with pastry, crimping edges. Make several slits in top of pastry and bake pie in a preheated 425° oven for 35 minutes or until top is golden.

119

PASTA, RICE & BEANS

COOKING PASTA

Serves 4 to 6
1 tablespoon salt
1 tablespoon cooking oil
1 pound fresh noodles, or
12 ounces dried noodles

Add salt and oil to 3 pints water and bring to a boil. Gradually add noodles and cook over medium heat, stirring occasionally, approximately 3 minutes for fresh, 8 minutes for dried noodles. Cook until just tender (al dente). Serve with any of the following sauces.

Chinese Noodles One pound of fresh Chinese noodles or 1/2 pound dried Chinese noodles may be cooked by the above method.

ANCHOVY SAUCE

generous 1/4 pint olive oil
2 cloves garlic, crushed
2 2-ounce cans anchovy fillets
4 fresh mint leaves, finely chopped
4 tablespoons chopped parsley
2 tablespoons capers
10 pitted black olives, chopped
freshly ground pepper to taste

In a frying pan, heat oil. Add garlic; sauté until garlic is brown and discard. Add anchovies to oil and cook, stirring until they dissolve into a paste. Remove from heat and blend in remaining ingredients. Toss with freshly cooked pasta and serve immediately.

PASTA, RICE & BEANS

TOMATO SAUCE, NEAPOLITAN STYLE

scant 1/2 pint olive oil
3 cloves garlic, crushed
2 pounds ripe tomatoes, peeled, seeded and chopped
2 tablespoons chopped basil, or
2 teaspoons dried basil
2 tablespoons chopped parsley
salt and freshly ground pepper to taste

In a frying pan, heat oil. Sauté garlic until brown; discard garlic and add tomatoes, basil, parsley, salt and pepper. Cook for 30 minutes over moderate heat. Toss with freshly cooked pasta and serve immediately.

OLIVE OIL, GARLIC AND CHILI SAUCE

scant 1/2 pint olive oil
3 to 4 cloves garlic, finely chopped
1 or more fresh green chili peppers, finely chopped, or
1/2 teaspoon or more crushed dried red Chili peppers
4 tablespoons chopped parsley
freshly ground pepper to taste

In a frying pan, heat oil. Add garlic, chilies and parsley; simmer 5 minutes. Toss with freshly cooked pasta and season with pepper. Serve immediately.

BACON SAUCE

2 tablespoons olive oil
1/2 pound lean bacon, diced
1 onion, sliced
3 large ripe tomatoes, peeled and chopped
1 teaspoon dried marjoram
salt and freshly ground pepper to taste
4 ounces grated Parmesan cheese

In a frying pan, heat oil. Fry bacon over low heat until fat is rendered; add onion and cook until transparent. Add tomatoes and marjoram and season with salt and pepper. Bring to a simmer and cook for 10 minutes. Toss with freshly cooked pasta and sprinkle with cheese. Serve immediately.

PRAWN AND TOMATO SAUCE

2 tablespoons olive oil
1 onion, chopped
2 garlic cloves, finely chopped
2 pounds tomatoes, peeled and chopped
1-1/2 pounds fresh prawns, shelled and deveined
1 tablespoon each chopped fresh basil, flat-leaf
    parsley and oregano
salt and freshly ground pepper to taste

Heat oil and sauté onion and garlic until soft and transparent. Add tomatoes and cook 15 minutes over medium heat. Add prawns, basil, parsley and oregano and cook 5 to 7 minutes longer or until prawns are just cooked through. Do not overcook. Season with salt and pepper. Toss with freshly cooked pasta.

PESTO

Serves 4 to 6
4 ounces fresh basil leaves, chopped
4 cloves garlic, very finely chopped
3 tablespoons finely chopped flat-leaf parsley
6 to 8 tablespoons pine nuts or walnuts (optional)
1/2 pint olive oil (or half butter, melted)
1/2 teaspoon salt
3 ounces grated Parmesan cheese

Crush basil, garlic cloves, parsley and pine nuts with a mortar and pestle to form a paste. Gradually stir in olive oil, salt and Parmesan. Toss with freshly cooked pasta and serve immediately.

SHEPHERD'S NOODLES

1/2 pound well-seasoned pork sausages
1 pound curd or cottage cheese
about 1/4 pint milk
2 ounces grated Parmesan cheese

Crumble the sausages in a frying pan. Sauté until browned. Remove from heat and blend in curd cheese and milk to form a thick sauce. Pour over freshly cooked pasta, sprinkle with cheese and serve immediately.

PASTA, RICE & BEANS

CHICKEN LIVER AND MUSHROOM SAUCE

1 pound chicken livers, quartered and dusted with
   flour seasoned with salt and freshly ground
   pepper to taste
6 tablespoons olive oil
1 clove garlic, finely chopped
1 onion, chopped
1/2 pound mushrooms, chopped
1 pound ripe tomatoes, peeled, seeded and
   chopped
1 6-ounce can tomato paste
1 tablespoon chopped basil, or
1 teaspoon dried basil
1 teaspoon dried oregano
1/4 teaspoon ground cinnamon
salt and cayenne pepper to taste
6 to 8 tablespoons dry red wine
grated Parmesan cheese

In a frying pan, sauté chicken livers in 3 tablespoons
olive oil. Remove from the pan and set aside.
Sauté garlic, onion and mushrooms in remaining
oil. Add remaining ingredients except cheese and
simmer for 1 hour, stirring occasionally. Mixture
should be smooth and slightly thickened. Return
livers to sauce and heat through. Pour over freshly
cooked pasta and sprinkle with cheese. Serve immediately.

SPAGHETTI WITH MARINARA SAUCE

3 tablespoons olive oil
1 large onion, finely chopped
4 cloves garlic, very finely chopped
1/2 pound mushrooms, chopped
2 pounds ripe tomatoes, peeled and chopped
2 tablespoons chopped basil
1/2 teaspoon dried oregano
1 teaspoon salt
1/4 teaspoon ground cinnamon
1 teaspoon sugar
1/4 teaspoon freshly ground pepper
3 anchovy fillets, chopped (optional)
grated Parmesan cheese

In a frying pan, heat oil. Sauté onions, garlic and
mushrooms until golden. Add tomatoes, basil,
oregano, salt, cinnamon, sugar and pepper and
cook for 10 minutes. Add anchovies and simmer 5
minutes. Toss with freshly cooked pasta and sprinkle with cheese. Serve immediately.

Variation with Italian Sausage Sauté 1/2 pound
Italian sausages (or well-seasoned pork sausages),
crumbled or sliced, with the onions, garlic and mushrooms.

NOODLES WITH BROCCOLI AND COTTAGE CHEESE

Serves 4
1/2 pound cottage cheese
1/2 pint sour cream
3/4 pound broccoli, cooked and chopped
4 tablespoons white wine
6 to 8 tablespoons chopped spring onions
1 teaspoon salt
1/2 teaspoon freshly ground pepper
1/2 teaspoon freshly grated nutmeg
1/2 pound egg noodles, cooked al dente
2 tablespoons grated Parmesan cheese
2 tablespoons butter

Combine all ingredients except noodles, Parmesan cheese and butter and mix thoroughly. Place noodles in a buttered 3-pint baking dish. Pour cheese sauce over the top, sprinkle with Parmesan and dot with butter. Bake in a preheated 350° oven for 30 minutes and serve immediately.

LASAGNE WITH CHICKEN AND CHEESE

Serves 4
12 ounces lasagne noodles (about 12 strips), cooked al dente
12 ounces, cooked chicken, finely chopped
8 ounces spinach, cooked and chopped
1/2 pound mozzarella cheese, grated
1/2 teaspoon aniseed, crushed
salt and freshly ground pepper to taste
generous 1/4 pint chicken stock

Butter a shallow baking dish and arrange 3 strips of lasagne noodles on bottom. Sprinkle one-third each of the chicken, spinach, cheese and seasoning over noodles. Repeat layers twice. Pour chicken stock over mixture, cover with aluminum foil and bake in a preheated 375° oven for 20 minutes. Remove foil and brown top under a preheated grill, if desired.

Variations Substitute for the chicken any of the following: turkey, ham, veal, pork, beef, sweetbreads, chicken livers, shrimps or prawns, crab, tuna, hard-boiled eggs.

PASTA, RICE & BEANS

HAM, PRAWNS AND RICE

Serves 4
1/4 pound shelled prawns, deveined and cut in
 half lengthwise
1/4 pound ham, diced
1 tablespoon soy sauce
1 tablespoon peanut oil
1 slice ginger root, finely chopped (optional)
2 cups (about 3/4 pound) rice, washed and well
 drained
1 green pepper, diced

Combine prawns, ham, soy sauce, peanut oil and
ginger root and let stand 10 minutes. Place rice in a
3-pint saucepan with a tight-fitting lid. Add 2-1/4
cups water, bring to a rapid boil and lower heat to
medium. When all of the water and bubbles have
disappeared from the surface of the rice, lower
heat to simmer. Place prawn and ham mixture on
top of rice, cover and cook 15 minutes. Add the
green pepper, cover and cook 5 minutes. Serve immediately.

Variation Add 2 fresh bean-curd cakes, diced, the
last 5 minutes of cooking. Bean curd is available
from Chinese stores.

CHICKEN AND RICE

Serves 4
1 pound boneless chicken, cut into thin strips
2 teaspoons sherry
1 tablespoon soy sauce
1 tablespoon peanut oil
1 or 2 slices ginger root, finely chopped
 (optional)
2 cups (about 12 ounces) rice, washed and well
 drained
1 pound fresh peas, shelled

Combine chicken, sherry, soy sauce, peanut oil and
ginger root and let stand 20 minutes. Place rice in a
3-pint saucepan with a tight-fitting lid. Add 2-1/4
cups water, bring to a rapid boil and lower heat to
medium. When all of the water and bubbles have
disappeared from the surface of the rice, lower
heat to simmer. Place chicken mixture on top of
rice, cover and cook 15 minutes. Add peas, cover
and cook 5 minutes. Serve immediately.

Variations Omit peas and add 4 ounces matchstick-
cut bamboo shoots or half bamboo shoots and half
water chestnuts the last 5 minutes of cooking.
Sprinkle with 4 tablespoons chopped spring onions
just before serving.

BEEF AND RICE

Serves 4
1 pound lean minced beef
6 to 8 tablespoons finely chopped water chestnuts
2 tablespoons soy sauce
1 tablespoon sherry
1 clove garlic, finely chopped
1 or 2 slices ginger root, finely chopped
   (optional)
2 cups (about 12 ounces) rice, washed and well
   drained
4 tablespoons chopped spring onions or fresh
   coriander

Combine beef, water chestnuts, soy sauce, sherry, garlic and ginger root and let stand 10 minutes. Place rice in a 3-pint saucepan with a tight-fitting lid. Add 2-1/4 cups water, bring to a rapid boil and lower heat to medium. When all of the water and bubbles have disappeared from the surface of the rice, lower heat to simmer. Place beef mixture on top of rice, cover and cook 20 minutes. Mix in spring onions and serve immediately.

Variations Add 4 ounces chopped carrots or green beans to the beef mixture.

PORK AND BEAN STEW

Serves 6
4 tablespoons olive oil
1 pound pork spareribs, cut into 3-inch lengths
1 pound spicy pork sausages
1 pound butter beans, washed, soaked overnight
   and drained
1 small Savoy cabbage (about 1 pound), shredded
4 ounces Florence fennel with leaves, chopped
2 onions, thinly sliced
2 large tomatoes, peeled and chopped
salt and freshly ground pepper to taste
accompaniments:
   crusty French or Italian bread
   grated Parmesan cheese

Heat oil in a flameproof casserole and fry spareribs until browned; add sausages and cook 5 minutes. Add beans, vegetables, salt, pepper and hot water to cover. Simmer for 1 hour or until beans are tender. Water may be added in small amounts as necessary. Serve hot with crusty bread and pass the grated cheese.

PASTA, RICE & BEANS

RED BEANS AND RICE

Serves 6

1 ham bone, cracked (so marrow will be released during cooking)
1 pound small dried red beans, washed, soaked overnight and drained
1 onion, chopped
3 cloves garlic, finely chopped
salt and freshly ground pepper to taste
accompaniments:
     freshly cooked rice
     chopped spring onions

Top-of-the-Stove Method
(large, heavy saucepan or soup pot may be used)

Place ham bone in a pot with 3 pints water. Bring to a boil and skim any surface scum. Add beans, onion and garlic. Reduce heat, cover and simmer for 2 hours or until beans are tender. Extra water may be added as needed during cooking period. Remove ham bone and mash some of the beans against the side of the pot to thicken the remaining liquid. Remove meat from the bone and return meat to the pot. Season with salt and pepper and serve with rice, topped with chopped spring onions.

Slow Cooker Method

Place beans in bottom of a slow cooker and add remaining ingredients, except rice and spring onions, with 2-1/2 pints water. Cover and cook on high 2 hours. Turn heat to low and cook, covered, 10 to 12 hours. Proceed as directed for top-of-the-stove method.

Pressure Cooker Method

Combine all ingredients except rice and spring onions, adding 4 pints of water or not more than two-thirds capacity. Cover and bring to full pressure. When steam appears, reduce heat and cook on low 20 minutes. Reduce pressure completely and let stand, covered, 10 to 15 minutes to blend flavors. Proceed as directed for top-of-the-stove method.

HAM HOCKS AND BUTTER BEANS

Serves 6

1 pound butter beans, washed, soaked overnight
  and drained
4 ham hocks, halved
2 bay leaves
1 onion, chopped
1 green pepper, chopped
1 pound ripe tomatoes, peeled and chopped
1/2 pint tomato juice
1 teaspoon sugar
1/4 teaspoon ground cloves
1/2 teaspoon freshly ground pepper
salt to taste

Top-of-the-Stove Method
Combine beans and 3 pints water in a large soup pot with remaining ingredients. Cover and simmer 1-1/2 hours or until beans and meat are tender.

Slow Cooker Method
Place beans in the bottom of a slow cooker and add remaining ingredients with 2-1/2 pints water. Cover and cook on high 2 hours. Turn heat to low and cook, covered, 10 to 12 hours.

Pressure Cooker Method
Combine all ingredients, adding 5 pints of water or not more than two-thirds capacity. Cover and bring to full pressure. When steam appears, reduce heat and cook on low 15 minutes. Reduce pressure completely and let stand, covered, 10 to 15 minutes to blend flavors.

PASTA, RICE & BEANS

BEANS WITH TUNA

Serves 6
5 tablespoons olive oil
1 clove garlic, crushed
1 pound small dried haricot beans, washed,
    soaked overnight and drained
1 pound ripe tomatoes, peeled and chopped
2 6-1/2-ounce cans white tuna, drained and
    separated into chunks
2 sprigs basil, finely chopped
salt and freshly ground pepper to taste

Top-of-the-Stove Method
In a heavy pan, heat oil and sauté garlic until
brown; discard garlic. Add beans and 3 pints
water, bring to a boil, reduce heat and simmer,
covered, for 1-1/2 hours or until beans are tender.
Add tomatoes, tuna, basil, salt and pepper. Simmer
for 20 minutes and serve immediately.

Slow Cooker Method
Sauté garlic in oil until brown in a frying pan or slow
cooker with a browning unit; discard garlic. Combine oil with beans and 2-1/2 pints water in a
slow cooker. Cover and cook on high 2 hours. Turn
heat to low, cover and cook 8 hours. Add remaining ingredients, cover and cook on high for 30
minutes.

LAMB SHANKS, SAUSAGES AND BEANS

Serves 4 to 6
2 onions, chopped
3 tablespoons butter
1 pound small dried haricot beans,
   washed, soaked overnight and drained
3 pounds shank end leg of lamb (2 to 3 shanks)
4 carrots, sliced
salt and freshly ground pepper to taste
1 bay leaf
4 garlic sausages, sliced diagonally 1/2 inch thick

Top-of-the-Stove Method

In a heavy pan, sauté onions in butter until transparent. Add remaining ingredients, except sausages, with 3 pints water. Bring to a boil, lower heat, cover and simmer 1-1/2 hours or until meat and beans are tender. Add sausages and simmer 20 minutes longer.

Slow Cooker Method

Place beans in bottom of a slow cooker and add remaining ingredients except sausages, with 2-1/2 pints water. Cover and cook on high 2 hours. Turn heat to low and cook, covered, 10 to 12 hours. Add sausages, cover and cook on high 20 minutes.

Pressure Cooker Method

In a pressure cooker sauté onions in butter until transparent. Add remaining ingredients except carrots and sausages, with 4 pints of water or not more than two-thirds capacity. Cover and bring to full pressure. When steam appears, reduce heat and cook on low 15 minutes. Reduce pressure completely, uncover, add carrots and sausages, cover and simmer 20 minutes, not under pressure.

PASTA, RICE & BEANS

PORK AND BEANS IN CREAM

Serves 6 to 8
1/2 pound salt pork, well rinsed and diced
1 onion, chopped
3 tablespoons butter
1 pound pink or kidney beans, washed, soaked
   overnight and drained
1 celery rib, chopped
1 bay leaf
1/2 pint double cream
2 egg yolks, beaten
salt and freshly ground pepper to taste
1/4 teaspoon freshly grated nutmeg
garnish: chopped parsley

Top-of-the-Stove Method
In a large pan, sauté the salt pork and onion in butter for 5 minutes. Add the beans, celery and bay leaf with 3 pints water. Bring to a boil, skimming off any surface scum. Cover with a tight-fitting lid, lower heat and simmer 1-1/2 hours or until beans are tender. Combine cream, egg yolks, salt, pepper and nutmeg and add to beans. Simmer for 5 minutes or until thickened. Sprinkle with parsley and serve.

Slow Cooker Method
Sauté salt pork and onion in butter in a frying pan or a slow cooker with a browning unit for 5 minutes. Combine with the beans, celery and bay leaf and 2-1/2 pints water in a slow cooker. Cover and cook on high 2 hours. Turn heat to low and cook, covered, 10 to 12 hours. Combine cream, egg yolks, salt and pepper and nutmeg and add to pot. Cook on high, uncovered, 5 minutes or until thickened. Sprinkle with parsley and serve.

Pressure Cooker Method
In a pressure cooker sauté the salt pork and onion in butter for 5 minutes. Add the beans, celery, bay leaf and 4 pints of water or not more than two-thirds capacity. Cover and bring to full pressure, reduce heat and cook on low 15 minutes. Reduce pressure completely and let stand, covered, 10 to 15 minutes to blend flavors. Combine cream, egg yolks, salt, pepper and nutmeg and add to beans. Simmer, uncovered and not under pressure, 5 minutes or until thickened. Sprinkle with parsley and serve.

OXTAILS AND CHICK PEAS, ITALIAN STYLE

Serves 4 to 6
2 cloves garlic, finely chopped
1 onion, chopped
3 tablespoons olive oil
3 pounds oxtails, disjointed, parboiled 5
     minutes and drained
3/4 pint beef stock
4 ounces Florence fennel, including tops,
     chopped
1/2 teaspoon dried oregano
salt and freshly ground pepper to taste
4 ounces cooked ham, diced
4 ounces chick peas, cooked
accompaniment: tossed green salad

Top-of-the-Stove Method
(flameproof casserole or heavy saucepan may be used)
Sauté garlic and onion in olive oil until onion is transparent. Add oxtails and cook until browned. Add stock, fennel, oregano, salt and pepper. Cover and simmer 1-1/2 hours or until tender. Add ham and chick peas and cook 20 minutes. Serve with a green salad.

Slow Cooker Method
Sauté garlic and onion in oil in a frying pan or a slow cooker with a browning unit. Add oxtails and cook until browned. Combine all ingredients except ham and chick peas in a slow cooker, cover and cook on low 8 to 10 hours. Add ham and chick peas, cover and cook on high 20 minutes. Serve with a green salad.

Pressure Cooker Method
In a pressure cooker sauté the onion and garlic in oil until onions are transparent. Add oxtails and cook until browned. Add all remaining ingredients except the ham and chick peas, with 1/2 pint water. Cover and bring to full pressure. When steam appears, reduce heat and cook on low 30 minutes. Reduce pressure completely and add ham and chick peas. Cover and cook for 20 minutes, not under Serve with a green salad.

Wet Clay Cooker Method
Combine all ingredients except ham and chick peas, reducing stock by a quarter. Place in a pre-soaked unglazed clay cooker, cover and place in a cold oven. Turn oven to 400° and bake 1-1/2 hours or until tender. Add the ham and chick peas, cover and bake 20 minutes. Remove from oven and let stand 10 minutes. Serve with a green salad.

TABLETOP COOKERY

One-pot cookery achieves its most festive form in tabletop cooking. For entertaining, these recipes are a boon to the otherwise harassed hostess/cook. With a chafing dish or fondue pot she may now feed her guests without leaving the table.

True tabletop cooking was more widely practised in the Orient than in Europe. The Chinese actually invented the hibachi, though it is now more associated with Japanese cooking in numerous grilled teriyaki dishes and the nabemono (meal in a pot) tradition. The hibachi is a portable charcoal grill consisting of a heavy iron pot filled with glowing charcoal, with a grid laid over the top. However, most dining rooms lack adequate ventilation for the hibachi to be used indoors and so it is best left for outdoor use.

Europe's contributions to tabletop cookery are the chafing dish and fondue pot. Classically these were used as warming dishes, rather than actual cooking pots. (The French term for chafing dish is *réchaud,* to re-warm.) In turn-of-the-century America, restaurant chefs began competing for dramatic dishes cooked and often flambéed at the table. By mid-century a chafing dish was virtually a staple in every middle-class household, only to be displaced by the fondue craze of the 1960's.

You don't, however, need specialized pots for tabletop cookery. An electric frying pan or a frying pan placed over a hot plate may be used in place of a fondue pot or chafing dish.

TABLETOP COOKERY

PRAWNS AND RICE

Serves 4
3 tablespoons butter
1 onion, chopped
1 fresh green chili pepper, seeded and finely
  chopped, or
1/2 teaspoon crushed dried red chili peppers
6 to 8 tablespoons chopped sweet green pepper
4 tablespoons chopped parsley
1/2 pound ripe tomatoes, peeled and chopped
1 cup (about 6 ounces) long-grain rice
1/2 pound shelled medium-size prawns
4 ounces cooked ham, diced
garnish: 6 to 8 tablespoons chopped spring
  onions

Heat butter in the top pan (blazer) of a chafing dish placed directly over the flame and sauté onion, chili pepper and sweet pepper until vegetables are limp. Add parsley and tomatoes, bring to a boil, then add rice and 1 cup hot water. Return to boil and stir in prawns and ham. Cover, place top pan over the hot water pan (lower pan) and let steam 20 minutes or until rice is tender. Garnish with chopped spring onions.

PRAWNS NEWBURG

Serves 4 to 6
2 shallots, finely chopped
4 tablespoons butter
3/4 pound shelled medium-size prawns
1/2 teaspoon paprika
pinch of cayenne pepper
6 to 8 tablespoons Madeira or sherry
1/2 pint milk
4 tablespoons double cream
4 egg yolks, well beaten
1 tablespoon brandy
salt and white pepper to taste
garnish: 2 tablespoons finely chopped parsley
accompaniment: freshly cooked rice or
  freshly made toast

In the top pan (blazer) of a chafing dish placed directly over a low flame, sauté the shallots in butter for 1 minute. Add the prawns and cook over a brisk fire until prawns become pink, about 3 minutes. Add paprika, cayenne and Madeira and cook until wine is reduced by half. Place the top pan over the hot water pan (lower pan). Blend milk and cream with egg yolks and gradually add to prawn mixture. Stirring constantly to prevent curdling, cook until thickened. Add brandy, salt and pepper. Garnish with parsley and serve over rice or toast.

SHELLFISH STEW, CHILEAN STYLE

Serves 6
6 tablespoons butter
1 onion, chopped
4 tablespoons flour
1-1/2 pints fish stock or clam juice, heated
3/4 pint dry white wine
1/2 teaspoon white pepper
1/2 pound shelled medium-size prawns, deveined
    and halved lengthwise
1 pound scallops, halved or quartered
1 or more fresh green chili peppers, seeded and
    finely chopped, or
1/2 teaspoon crushed dried red chili peppers
1/2 pint double cream
2 hard-boiled eggs, chopped
6 to 8 tablespoons slivered blanched almonds
salt and freshly ground pepper to taste
accompaniment: crusty French rolls

Heat butter in the top pan (blazer) of a chafing
dish placed directly over the flame and sauté onion
until transparent. Blend in flour and cook 2 minutes. Add stock, wine and white pepper and simmer 20 minutes. Then add prawns, scallops and
chili peppers and cook 5 to 7 minutes or until
seafood is done. Add cream and eggs; heat through.
Stir in almonds, salt and pepper. Accompany with
French rolls.

CAPE COD FISH CHOWDER

Serves 6
1/4 pound salt pork, well rinsed and diced
2 onions, thinly sliced
1-1/2 pounds potatoes, peeled and diced
1 celery rib with leaves, diced
2 pounds cod, halibut or other firm white fish
    fillets, cut into 1-inch pieces
3/4 pint milk
salt and freshly ground pepper to taste
2 tablespoons butter
accompaniment: salty crackers

In the top pan (blazer) of a chafing dish placed
directly over the flame, sauté salt pork until fat is
rendered. Add onions and cook until transparent;
add potatoes, celery and 1-1/2 pints boiling water.
Cover and cook 10 minutes; add fish and cook 10
minutes. Add milk, salt, pepper and butter, heat
through and serve with crackers.

TABLETOP COOKERY

EGGS RANCHEROS

Serves 4 to 6
2 tablespoons olive oil
1 clove garlic, finely chopped
1 onion, chopped
1 small sweet green pepper, finely chopped
1/4 teaspoon crushed dried red chili peppers
1 pound ripe tomatoes, peeled, seeded and
  chopped
1/2 teaspoon dried oregano
1/4 teaspoon ground cumin
6 eggs
accompaniment: warm tortillas (page 101) or
  freshly made toast

Heat the oil in the top pan (blazer) of a chafing dish placed directly over the flame. Sauté garlic and onion until transparent. Add the peppers, tomatoes, oregano and cumin and bring to a boil. Break eggs one at a time onto a saucer, slip into tomato mixture and poach 3 minutes or until whites are set. Yolks should remain soft. Serve with tortillas or toast.

ASPARAGUS FRITTATA

Serves 4
3 tablespoons olive oil
1 clove garlic, very finely chopped
1 onion, thinly sliced
1 pound asparagus tips, thinly sliced on the
  diagonal
1/2 teaspoon dried oregano
1/2 teaspoon salt
1/4 teaspoon freshly ground pepper
6 eggs, beaten
6 to 8 tablespoons grated Parmesan cheese
accompaniment: French or Italian bread

Heat oil in the top pan (blazer) of a chafing dish placed directly over the flame and sauté garlic and onion until transparent. Add asparagus and oregano, cover and cook 3 minutes or until asparagus are tender-crisp. Add salt and pepper to eggs and pour over asparagus, stirring once. When eggs begin to set, sprinkle cheese on top. Slip out onto a platter and cut into wedges. Serve with crusty French bread.

FETTUCCINE

Serves 4 to 6
1/4 pound butter
1/2 pint milk, mixed with
4 tablespoons double cream
1 pound fresh fettuccine noodles or egg noodles,
    cooked al dente and kept warm
6 ounces Parmesan cheese (or half Pecorino
    cheese), grated
freshly grated nutmeg
salt and freshly ground pepper to taste
accompaniments: antipasto platter composed of
    any combination of the following: anchovy
    fillets, Italian salami, marinated mushrooms or
    artichokes, tiny tomatoes, celery sticks,
    olives, mild pepperoni, radishes, etc.

In the top pan (blazer) of a chafing dish placed
directly over the flame, heat butter and half of the
milk mixture. Bring just to a boil, add noodles,
tossing lightly with a pair of forks. Sprinkle in
cheese and continue to toss noodles, gradually adding remaining creamy milk. Add nutmeg, salt and
pepper and serve immediately.

SCRAMBLED EGGS AND SMOKED SALMON

Serves 4
6 eggs
3 tablespoons creamy milk
3 tablespoons chopped chives
3 tablespoons butter
8 slices smoked salmon
8 slices buttered rye toast

Beat together eggs, creamy milk and chives. Melt
butter in top pan (blazer) of a chafing dish placed
directly over the flame. Add egg mixture and stir
until eggs begin to set; do not overcook. Place a
slice of salmon on each piece of toast and top with
scrambled eggs. Serve immediately.

TABLETOP COOKERY

BEER SAUSAGES

Serves 4
1 pound pork sausages
1/2 pint beer
accompaniments:
    tart crisp apples, sliced, or
    pickles and sliced tomatoes
    rye bread and butter
    beer to drink

Prick sausages and cook until brown in the top pan (blazer) of a chafing dish placed directly over the flame. Pour off all drippings and add beer and continue cooking until beer has been reduced by half. Serve with accompaniments.

WELSH RAREBIT

Serves 4 to 6
2 tablespoons butter
1 pound Cheddar cheese, grated
1/2 pint beer or ale, at room temperature
1/2 teaspoon paprika
1/2 teaspoon dry mustard
freshly made toast

Melt the butter in the top pan (blazer) of a chafing dish placed over hot water pan (lower pan). Add the cheese; when it begins to melt, slowly add the beer or ale, stirring constantly. Season with paprika and mustard and cook for 5 minutes. Lower heat and keep warm until ready to serve over hot toast.

CHILI RAREBIT

Serves 6
3 tablespoons butter
1 small onion, finely chopped
1 clove garlic, finely chopped
1 or more fresh green chili peppers, seeded and
    chopped, or
1/2 teaspoon or more crushed dried red chili
    peppers
2 tablespoons flour
1/2 pint milk
6 ounces Cheddar cheese, grated
3/4 pound ripe tomatoes, peeled and chopped
1/2 teaspoon salt
1/4 teaspoon freshly ground pepper
2 egg yolks, well beaten
accompaniment: toasted French bread

Melt the butter in the top pan (blazer) of a chafing dish placed directly over a low flame and sauté the onion, garlic and chilies until onion is transparent. Place the top pan over hot water pan (lower pan), add the flour and blend well. Gradually add the milk, stirring constantly until smooth and thickened. Add the cheese and continue stirring until melted. Add tomatoes, salt and pepper and cook for 10 minutes. Blend 1/4 pint of hot mixture with the egg yolks and return to the pan. Continue cooking and stirring for 2 minutes. Serve with toasted French bread.

Variation Add 1/2 pound diced cooked chicken to the sauce when adding egg yolks.

TABLETOP COOKERY

BAGNA CAUDA

Serves 4
1/4 pound butter
6 tablespoons olive oil
4 cloves garlic, finely chopped
1 2-ounce can anchovy fillets, chopped
6 celery ribs, cut into sticks
3 green peppers, cut into wide strips
4 medium-sized artichokes, cooked
1 cauliflower, broken into flowerets
3 courgettes, cut into sticks
8 spring onions
8 whole mushrooms
6 fennel stalks
accompaniment: Italian or French bread

Heat butter and oil in the top pan (blazer) of a chafing dish placed directly over the flame and sauté garlic; do not brown. Remove from heat and add anchovies, stirring well. Return pan to low heat and continue cooking until anchovies have dissolved into a paste. Serve vegetables on individual plates for dipping into garlic-anchovy sauce. Accompany with Italian or French bread.

CURRY OF LAMB

Serves 4
2 tablespoons butter
4 tablespoons chopped onion
1 tart apple, peeled and chopped
1 tablespoon flour
1 tablespoon curry powder
3/4 pint lamb or chicken stock
1 egg yolk, beaten
1 tablespoon fresh lemon juice
3/4 pound diced cooked lamb
salt and freshly ground pepper to taste
accompaniment:
   freshly cooked rice
   chutney, chopped toasted cashews

Melt butter in top pan (blazer) of a chafing dish placed directly over the flame and sauté onion and apple over a brisk fire until golden. Add flour and curry powder and cook 2 minutes. Stir in stock and cook until smooth and thickened, about 5 minutes. Reduce flame to low, remove 1/4 pint of the sauce and combine with egg yolk and lemon juice. Return to pan, add lamb, season with salt and pepper and heat through. Serve immediately with rice and accompaniments.

Variation Substitute cooked prawns for the lamb and use chicken stock.

MEATBALL CURRY

Serves 6 to 8
Meatballs
1 pound minced lamb
1/2 pound minced veal
1 onion, finely chopped
1 egg, beaten
1 teaspoon salt
1/2 teaspoon freshly ground pepper
2 tablespoons chopped coriander or parsley

Sauce
3 tablespoons butter
1 onion, thinly sliced
3 tablespoons flour
1 tablespoon curry powder
2 teaspoons sugar
1-1/2 pints tomato juice
pinch of cayenne pepper

accompaniments:
    freshly cooked rice
    chutney
    chopped roasted peanuts
    finely chopped spring onions

Combine all the ingredients for meatballs and make walnut-sized balls. Set aside. For the sauce, heat butter in the top pan (blazer) of a chafing dish placed directly over the flame and sauté onion until transparent. Blend in flour and curry powder and cook 2 minutes. Add sugar, tomato juice and cayenne, stirring until slightly thickened. Add meatballs and cook 20 minutes. Serve over rice with accompaniments.

TABLETOP COOKERY

CHICKEN AND OYSTER MEDLEY, SOUTHERN STYLE

Serves 4 to 6
2 slices bacon, diced
2 tablespoons butter
1/2 pound diced cooked chicken
2 large tomatoes, peeled, seeded and chopped
1 small onion, chopped
1 green pepper, chopped
1/4 pound fresh or frozen corn kernels
1/4 pound okra, sliced
1/4 pound small young broad beans
pinch of cayenne pepper
1 dozen oysters, with their liquor
salt and white pepper to taste

In the top pan (blazer) of a chafing dish placed directly over the flame, sauté the bacon until the fat is rendered but the bacon is not crisp. Add butter, chicken, all the vegetables and the cayenne. Cover the chafing dish and cook for 10 minutes. Uncover and add the oysters; salt and pepper lightly. Cover and cook for 7 minutes or until oysters are just heated through. Serve immediately.

BARBECUED BEEF

Serves 6
3 tablespoons bacon drippings
3 onions, thinly sliced
2 cloves garlic, finely chopped
2 celery ribs with leaves, finely chopped
1 teaspoon dry mustard
1 teaspoon compound chili powder
3 tablespoons brown sugar
1 teaspoon salt
1/2 teaspoon freshly ground pepper
3 to 4 tablespoons vinegar
6 to 8 tablespoons dry white wine
3/4 pint tomato juice
1 pound cooked roast beef, cut into thin strips
garnish: chopped spring onions (optional)
accompaniment: buns or freshly made toast

Heat bacon drippings in the top pan (blazer) of a chafing dish placed directly over the flame and sauté onions and garlic until transparent. Add celery and cook 5 minutes. Add remaining ingredients, except beef, place top pan over hot water pan (lower pan) and simmer for 25 minutes. Add beef and heat through, about 5 minutes. Serve garnished with spring onions on buns or toast.

Variations Substitute cooked venison, roast pork, chicken or turkey for the roast beef.

SAUTÉED CHICKEN LIVERS AND BACON

Serves 4 to 6
3 slices bacon, diced
1 pound chicken livers, dredged in
2 tablespoons flour
4 tablespoons chopped onion
4 tablespoons chopped green pepper
1/2 teaspoon dried tarragon
6 to 8 tablespoons dry red wine
2 ounces black olives, pitted
4 tablespoons chopped parsley
salt and freshly ground pepper to taste
accompaniment: hot toast, muffins or waffles

In the top pan (blazer) of a chafing dish placed directly over the flame, sauté the bacon until the fat is rendered. Add the livers to the pan and cook for 3 minutes, turning the livers frequently until browned. Add the onion and pepper and cook 2 minutes. Add tarragon and wine and cook 5 minutes. Add olives, parsley, salt and pepper. Heat through and serve on hot toast, muffins or waffles.

Variation Substitute sliced lamb or veal kidneys for chicken livers.

VEAL KIDNEYS, FLAMBÉED

Serves 4
3 tablespoons butter
4 veal kidneys, cut into 1/4-inch-thick slices
1/4 pound button mushrooms, sliced
2 shallots, finely chopped
5 tablespoons brandy, warmed
1/2 teaspoon dry mustard
salt and freshly ground pepper to taste
scant 1/2 pint double cream
garnish: 2 tablespoons chopped parsley
accompaniment: freshly made toast or vol-au-
    vent cases

In the top pan (blazer) of a chafing dish placed directly over the flame, melt the butter and sauté the kidneys, mushrooms and shallots over a brisk fire for 5 minutes or until kidneys are brown. Add the warmed brandy and ignite; when the flame burns out, add the mustard, salt, pepper and cream and heat through. Garnish with parsley and serve immediately over toast or in vol-au-vent cases.

TABLETOP COOKERY

CREAMED TURKEY AND MUSHROOMS

Serves 4
4 ounces button mushrooms, sliced
2 tablespoons chopped onion
2 tablespoons butter
1 tablespoon flour
1/4 pint milk, mixed with
4 tablespoons double cream
2 eggs, beaten
4 tablespoons Madeira or sherry
3/4 pound cooked turkey, diced
2 tablespoons chopped parsley
pinch of freshly grated nutmeg
salt and freshly ground pepper to taste
accompaniments:
   hot buttered toast or freshly cooked rice
   slivered toasted almonds

In the top pan (blazer) of a chafing dish placed directly over the flame, sauté the mushrooms and onion in butter for 3 minutes; add the flour and cook and stir 1 minute. Gradually add milk mixture and continue stirring until smooth and thickened. Place the top pan over the hot water pan (lower pan). Blend 1/4 pint of the hot mixture with the beaten eggs and return to the pan. Continue to cook, stirring constantly, for 2 minutes. Add Madeira, turkey, parsley, nutmeg, salt and pepper and heat through. Serve over toast or rice and top with almonds.

Variations
• Substitute cooked flaked crab meat for turkey, adding it at the same time as Madeira.
• Substitute 2 7-ounce cans of tuna, drained, for turkey, adding it at the same time as Madeira; omit salt and add 4 to 6 ounces fresh, cooked peas, if desired.

FONDUE DIPPING SAUCES

Curry Sauce
4 tablespoons fresh lemon juice
1/2 teaspoon salt
1 teaspoon curry powder
pinch of cayenne pepper
1 large egg
1/2 pint peanut or corn oil

Combine all ingredients except oil in a blender and blend for 10 seconds. Gradually add the oil and blend until thick and smooth.

Lemon Mayonnaise
4 tablespoons fresh lemon juice
1 strip lemon peel
1/2 pint mayonnaise
1 spring onion, cut up
1 clove garlic

Combine all ingredients in a blender and blend until smooth. Chill until ready to use.

Horseradish Sauce
1/2 pint sour cream
1 tablespoon prepared horseradish
1 teaspoon fresh lemon juice

Combine all ingredients in a blender and blend until smooth. Chill until ready to use.

Flavored Butters
Garlic butter Soften 1/4 pound butter and blend in 1 or 2 cloves garlic, finely chopped.
Tarragon butter Soften 1/4 pound butter and blend in 1 tablespoon finely chopped fresh tarragon or 1 teaspoon dried tarragon.
Blue cheese butter Soften 1/4 pound butter and blend in 4 tablespoons crumbled blue cheese.
Anchovy butter Soften 1/4 pound butter and blend in 2 anchovy fillets, mashed, or 2 tablespoons anchovy paste.

TABLETOP COOKERY

SWISS FONDUE

Serves 4 to 6
1 clove garlic
3/4 pint dry white wine
1-1/2 pounds Emmenthal or Gruyère cheese,
   grated or cut into small cubes
2 teaspoons cornflour, mixed with
4 tablespoons kirsch
pinch of freshly ground pepper
pinch of freshly grated nutmeg
French bread, cut into 1-inch cubes
accompaniments:
   green salad or fresh fruit for dessert
   a dry white wine, such as Riesling

Rub the inside of a fondue pot or blazer (top pan) of a chafing dish with the garlic clove, then discard garlic. Heat the wine in the pot placed over flame and add cheese, stirring constantly until smooth. When bubbles begin to appear, add the cornflour and kirsch mixture. Season with pepper and nutmeg. Fondue should be kept slightly bubbling while cooking. Spear bread cubes with a fondue fork, roll in fondue and eat. Serve with a green salad or fresh fruit for dessert and white wine.

BEEF FONDUE

Serves 4 to 6
peanut or corn oil
2 pounds tender beef steak, such as fillet or sirloin,
   cut into 1-inch cubes
accompaniments:
   various condiments and sauces such as horse-
      radish, mustard, Tabasco, Curry Sauce,
      Lemon Mayonnaise, anchovy, garlic or blue
      cheese butter, page 147
   French bread
   chopped onions, sliced tomatoes and pickles

Fill a fondue pot or chafing dish to no more than one-half full with oil. Place over flame and heat to 375° or until a cube of bread or meat sizzles upon contact with oil. Spear meat with fondue fork and cook to desired doneness in the oil. Transfer to another fork, dip in accompanying sauces and eat with remaining accompaniments. Do not eat from fondue fork as it may burn your mouth.

Variations A mixture of various meats and seafood may be used, such as lamb, veal, chicken breast, prawns, scallops, oysters, salmon or turbot.

BROTH FONDUE

Serves 4 to 6
1-1/2 pints chicken stock
1/2 pint dry white wine
1 tablespoon finely chopped fresh tarragon, or
1 teaspoon dried tarragon
4 tablespoons finely chopped spring onions
1/4 teaspoon freshly ground pepper
2 pounds tender beef steak, such as fillet
　or sirloin, cut into 1-inch cubes
brandy (optional)
accompaniments:
　French bread
　various seasonings or sauces for dipping, such
　　as mustard, ketchup, horseradish, Worcester-
　　shire sauce, Tabasco, pickles and onions

In a fondue pot, chafing dish or firepot, combine
all the ingredients except meat and brandy and
simmer for 15 minutes. Spear meat with fondue
fork and cook to desired doneness in broth. Serve
with accompaniments. When all meat has been
cooked, add a splash of brandy to stock, if desired,
and serve broth in individual cups.

Variations A mixture of various meats or seafood
may be used, such as chicken breast, lamb, prawns,
scallops, oysters or firm fish fillets.

TABLETOP COOKERY

SHABU SHABU

Serves 6 to 8

2 pounds lean tender beef steak, such as fillet
   or sirloin, sliced 1/8 inch thick
1 pound Chinese cabbage, leaves separated and
   halved if large
1 bunch spinach or watercress, tough stems
   removed
2 carrots, cut diagonally into thin slices
8 spring onions, cut into 4-inch lengths
1 pound fresh bean-curd cakes, cut into
   1-inch cubes*
1/2 pound button mushrooms
3 to 3-1/2 pints chicken stock
accompaniment: freshly cooked rice (optional)
assorted sauces and condiments:
   Lemon and Soy Sauce, following
   Sesame and Soy Sauce, following
   seeded and crushed small dried red chili peppers
   grated ginger root
   finely chopped spring onions

Prepare meat and vegetables and arrange on large platters; place sauces and condiments in bowls. Surround cooking pot with the platters and bowls. Provide each diner with a plate, a rice bowl, a pair of chopsticks to hold the foods while they are cooking, small bowls for dipping sauces and soup bowls or cups. Place the stock in a firepot or the top pan (blazer) of a chafing dish placed directly over the flame. When stock is bubbling, each diner selects foods from the platters with his chopsticks and cooks them in the stock until they are done to his preference. The foods are then eaten with the sauces and condiments. When all cooking is done, serve broth in cups or bowls.

*Available in Oriental stores.

Lemon and Soy Sauce Combine equal parts Japanese soy sauce and fresh lemon juice.

Sesame and Soy Sauce Combine 8 tablespoons toasted sesame seeds, ground, 4 tablespoons each Japanese soy sauce and mirin (Japanese sweet rice wine) or sherry and 1 tablespoon sugar.

weights and measures

The recipes in this book were originally devised and tested using American cup and spoon measures. These have been converted to fractions of pounds, ounces and pints where it seemed most practical. However, in some cases, where comparative volumes are more important to the success of a dish, the original cup measures have been retained.

The American cup holds 8 fluid ounces, the equivalent of a medium-sized teacup, and 2 cups, or 16 fluid ounces, make 1 American pint. (The Imperial pint holds

20 fluid ounces, or one-fifth more, and whenever pints have been used it is the 20-ounce pint that is meant.) However, provided the same cup is used throughout a recipe, a slight discrepancy will not matter. What is important is that cups, tablespoons and teaspoons should always be measured level.

For those who wish to use metric measures, the equivalents, adjusted to the nearest con-venient figure, are as follows (volume and weight).

Should you wish to make a more accurate conversion (particularly useful for baking, etc.), the exact equivalents are:

1 ounce	=	28.35 grammes
16 ounces	=	453.6 grammes
1 pint	=	568 millilitres
1 kilo	=	2.2 pounds
1 litre	=	1.76 pints
1 decilitre	=	100 millilitres

OUNCES/FLUID OUNCES		GRAMMES/MILLILITRES
½	=	15
1	=	25
2	=	50
3	=	75
4 (¼ pound)	=	100–110
5 (¼ pint)	=	150 (1½ decilitres)
6	=	175
7	=	200 (2 decilitres)
8 (½ pound)	=	225 (use ¼ kilo)
9	=	250 (2½ decilitres = ¼ kilo)
10 (½ pint)	=	275 (use 2½ decilitres)
11	=	300 (3 decilitres)
12	=	350 (3½ decilitres)
13	=	375
14	=	400 (4 decilitres)
15 (¾ pint)	=	425 (4½ decilitres)
16 (1 pound)	=	450 (4½ decilitres)
17	=	475
18	=	500 (5 decilitres = ½ kilo)
19	=	550 (5½ decilitres)
20 (1 pint)	=	575 (use 5½ decilitres)

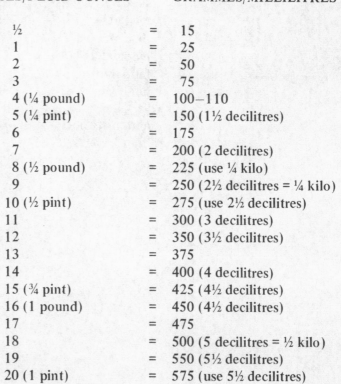

The oven temperatures in this book are given in °F. Gas Regulo and Celsius (Centigrade) equivalents are as follows:

	FAHRENHEIT		GAS MARK		CELSIUS
very cool	225	=	¼	=	110
very cool	250	=	½	=	130
cool	275	=	1	=	140
very slow	300	=	2	=	150
slow	325	=	3	=	160
moderate	350	=	4	=	180
moderate	375	=	5	=	190
moderately hot	400	=	6	=	200
fairly hot	425	=	7	=	220
hot	450	=	8	=	230
very hot	475	=	9	=	240
extremely hot	500	=	10	=	250

Soup Pot

 Saucepan

 Slow Cooker

 Pressure Cooker

 Wet Clay Cooker

 Casserole

 Soufflé Dish

 Pie Dish

 Roasting Tin

 Baking Dish

 Frying Pan

 Chafing Dish

 Fondue Pot

INDEX

INDEX

INDEX

155

INDEX

156

INDEX

MARGARET GIN

Margaret Gin is the author of another title in the Pitman Home and Garden Series, *Offal; Gourmet Cookery from Head to Tail*. Mrs. Gin's Chinese ancestry, her girlhood in the southwestern United States, her travels to Europe and the many years she has resided in San Francisco have given her a broad insight into the many ethnic cuisines whose recipes comprise this book. Between testing recipes and writing cookbooks, raising two teen-age sons, and entertaining frequently with her husband William in their homes in San Francisco and Napa Valley, multi-talented Margaret Gin works as a free-lance ski wear and fashion designer.

RIK OLSON

An artist versatile in many media, Rik Olson completed the drawings for this book after spending eight years in Europe as an arts and crafts instructor for the United States Army. While he was abroad, his graphics and photographs were widely exhibited in Germany and Italy, winning a number of awards in Frankfurt and Florence. A native Californian, Rik Olson received his BFA degree from California College of Arts and Crafts and later studied photography in Germany and etching in Florence. He and his wife live in San Francisco.